Leveraging Your Financial Intelligence

At the Intersection of Money, Health, and Happiness

Doug Lennick, Roy Geer, and Ryan Goulart

WILEY

Library of Congress Cataloging-in-Publication Data is Available:

ISBN 9781119430780 (Hardcover)
ISBN 9781119430858 (ePDF)
ISBN 9781119430841 (ePub)

Cover Design: Wiley
Cover Image: © Juan Stockenstroom/Getty Images

Printed in the United States of America.

10 9 8 7 6 5 4 3 2 1

Contents

Preface

By Doug Lennick

It was nearly 43 years ago when I first met co-author Roy Geer. Roy passed away on March 8th, 2017, shortly before we had completed writing this book. You can imagine how sad this turn of events was. Roy would have been 90 years of age on his next birthday.

I was 22 when I first met Roy, and he was 47. Roy first became my mentor, and ultimately a friend and colleague. We shared a lot over the years, and one of the most important things we shared was a passion for making a difference. Our first book, *How to Get What You Want and Remain True to Yourself*, published in 1989, grew out of that passion. Several years ago, we decided it was time to work together on another book. Last year we realized our new book would be stronger if we added the perspective of a younger author, and that's when Ryan Goulart, a Millennial, joined the team as a co-author. Ryan, who had already been helping us with research, is now 29 years old. Among his many skills is a deep understanding of the Millennial generation's values, which in turn drive positive life choices; but even more important, Ryan shares our passion for making a difference. In addition, Ryan has deeply researched, and understands from personal experience, how Millennials experience the intersection of money, health, and happiness. As you'll see throughout this book, different generations—Millennials, Generation X, and Baby Boomers—have both similar and unique ways of optimizing happiness by leveraging financial intelligence to promote positive health and happiness practices.

Roy Geer was an inspiration for many, including Ryan and me. As Roy got older, he also got wiser. Roy knew how to age well, and that had a lot to do with knowing how to behave young. He remained an interested and active learner throughout his life. In fact, at the time of his death Roy was not only working on this book, but he was also in the process of completing the requirements for his PhD. For decades I had thought Roy had a PhD in industrial psychology, and he didn't correct my assumption quickly. About 10 years ago, feeling guilty, Roy admitted to me that he didn't have a PhD, but that he was inspired—in part by my mistaken belief—to pursue his doctorate. Though Roy didn't complete his PhD before he left us, I believe that his PhD studies greatly enhanced his happiness, longevity, and purpose. Richard Leider, bestselling author of *The Power of Purpose* and *Repacking Your Bags* (co-authored with David A. Shapiro), notes that "aging is changing" and that "purpose matters more." Leider speaks about "the language of living, not the language of aging." Words like *discovery, learning, opportunity, meaning,* and others represent the "language of living." Roy was all about that, and so is this book.

Our subtitle, *At the Intersection of Money, Health, and Happiness,* sets the stage for what you are about to experience. Research and the individual experiences of the authors and the many people we have coached or interviewed led us to conclude that indeed there is a clear connection between one's financial well-being, one's physical well-being, and one's happiness. As is true with the chicken and the egg, it is hard to know which comes first, but happiness expert Dan Buettner of Blue Zone fame states, "When it comes to health and wealth and happiness, it's hard to be happy if you don't have good health." We certainly agree with that, though there are many heartening examples of people facing extraordinary health challenges who, despite their circumstances, demonstrate remarkable emotional resilience, find joy in life, and spread positive energy to those around them. We also know that it's harder to be healthy if one is under financial stress, which countless studies and surveys indicate that up to 90 percent of Americans experience. Hence the significance of the title *Leveraging Your Financial Intelligence: At the Intersection of Money, Health, and Happiness.* Happiness may be one's ultimate goal, but we believe the fastest way to achieve happiness is to begin reducing financial stress by using the strategies presented in this book.

My book, *Financial Intelligence: Making Smart, Values-Based Decisions with Your Money and Your Life,* written several years ago with the support of my long-time, incredible collaborative writer, Kathy Jordan, was designed to help people understand and develop financial intelligence. Financial intelligence is "the ability to make smart, responsible, values-based decisions with and about money in the face of competing and difficult to deal with emotions." *Leveraging Your Financial Intelligence: Making Smart, Values-Based Decisions with Your Money and Your Life* is exactly what it says. When you leverage your financial intelligence, you create your own intersection of money, health, and happiness. We've had the privilege of knowing many people who have leveraged their financial intelligence to support financial, physical, and emotional well-being.

For example, consider Moses (Moe) Smith, a chiropractor and business owner who is financially intelligent:

> *I knew I wanted a job that gave me the opportunity to make unlimited income. I learned both how to be a chiropractor and how to be a business-woman. I want to know what's going on. I can tell you within $10 at any point in time what's in my checking, savings, and investment accounts. There are only two options: You're either stressed out about money or you aren't. I know too many people who are smart and end up broke.*

Moe is both smart and not broke. She is also generally not stressed out about money, which has contributed both to her physical health and her happiness. As Moe puts it, "When I get stressed financially or otherwise, I stop exercising. I have to combat that all of the time." That's why Moe decided to become financially intelligent, and that's why she is able to leverage her financial intelligence and create her own intersection of money, health, and happiness.

Marjorie and John Wynn are also financially intelligent. Their circumstances are different from Smith's, yet they are financially intelligent nonetheless. Marjorie and John are successful executives and exceptional parents. Marjorie is a marketing executive, and John is a technology executive. Although Marjorie and John make joint financial decisions with the help of their financial advisor, they decided Marjorie should handle all the day-to-day financial responsibilities. John is proud and grateful that "Marjorie takes on the vast majority of the financial issues."

Marjorie and John live in a beautiful home and neighborhood in Woodbury, Minnesota, a suburb on the east side of St. Paul, Minnesota. When Marjorie and John moved into their home years ago, it was a financial stretch. But as Marjorie put it, "I thought we should invest more for the home and the neighborhood where we would raise our family and where our children would have access to excellent public schools." This decision to invest in a high-end area was a values-based decision. It was inspired by their belief that where they lived would have a long-lasting impact on their children's success because of the educational, community, and cultural opportunities it would offer them. Meanwhile, Marjorie and John have saved and invested over the years so that they could ensure that their kids would have access to great college education options. This was another values-based decision. And those decisions have paid off: Their oldest daughter graduated from college and now has a job she loves located in the Twin Cities area. Their middle daughter now attends college at the University of Wisconsin. Their youngest is in high school and soon will be making her own college selection.

Another terrific example of financial intelligence comes from Tom and Michelle Young. As head of field distribution for Thrivent Financial, Young constantly works on enhancing his own, his employees', and Thrivent clients' financial intelligence. Michelle, who has been recognized as one of the nation's best financial advisors, and who currently works with Ameriprise Financial, does the same for herself and her clients. When it comes to their family's personal financial security, Tom said,

> Michelle and I are at a point where we need to reevaluate our life plans. I'm soon to be 41 and Michelle is almost 40, and we're raising three great kids. In the last number of years, we've been successful in setting goals for money, health, and happiness, and we are grateful that we've achieved our goals. The challenge we face now is that as we grow older and our family's needs evolve, we need to redefine goals for our next phase of life, based on our values and priorities.

Once Tom and Michelle identify their life goals going forward, that is where their intersection between money, health, and happiness will be.

What all of these individuals illustrate is that there are a number of different ways to express and leverage your financial intelligence. Our aim, and the intent of this book, is to help you do so in a way that works for you and, using the strategies presented in this book, will allow you to leverage your financial intelligence to create your own intersection of money, health, and happiness.

Acknowledgments

We begin with our families. If Roy Geer were still here to say it, he would lovingly express gratitude for the inspiration provided by his children, Rhonda, Rhea, and Russell; his grandchildren and great grandchildren; and his sons-in-law. Roy loved his family immensely and spoke of them often and proudly.

Ryan thanks his wife, Joanie, for supporting him through the countless extra hours it took to write this book. There were early hours and late hours and weekend hours, and Joanie was behind him no matter what. Ryan also appreciates the love, support, and guidance he has received all his life from his parents, Dorothy and Rick, and for the lessons learned growing up with his younger siblings, Jonathan and Audrey.

Doug knows his own life and career would not be where they are without the unfailing love and support of his wife, Beth Ann, who is a remarkable role model for healthy living and loving parenting. Doug is also grateful to his parents, who taught him the most important lessons we share in this book, and whose stories we hope will inspire readers to make smart decisions about finances, health, and happiness. In addition, Doug is thankful to be blessed with three wonderful children and their life partners, who have all chosen difference-making careers: Alan and his wife, Sari, Mary and her partner, LaCresia, and Joanie, who is married to co-author Ryan Goulart. Doug also finds regular inspiration from spending time with his grandson and best pal, Dylan.

The authors would like to acknowledge the extraordinary contribution of our collaborative writer, Kathy Jordan, PhD. *Leveraging Your Financial Intelligence: At the Intersection of Money, Health, and Happiness* is the fourth book Kathy has supported with co-author Doug, and the first book she has collaborated on with co-authors Ryan Goulart and Roy Geer. Kathy has a knack for capturing our voices, and the iterative process of working with her is engaging and results in the best book possible.

The authors would also like to acknowledge the research and literature review done by Alyssa Wynn and her sister, Samantha Wynn. Co-author Ryan coordinated their efforts, and we ended up with binders full of material that were extremely well organized and very well summarized, and that accelerated our progress in developing this book.

Of course, we appreciate greatly the many people we interviewed, from thought leaders and subject matter experts to people from all walks of life willing to share their stories with us and allow us to share their stories with all of you. The real-life stories of real people from their twenties to their seventies make the case for our message that indeed there is an intersection of money, health, and happiness.

Finally, we'd like to thank our colleagues. Roy worked throughout his life, and in later years conducted his consulting and coaching business as an independent practitioner. Before going solo he collaborated with his long-time partner, Bob Roberts. Ryan and Doug work together at think2perform with an incredibly talented group of people geographically spread throughout the country. They encourage you to visit think2perform.com and acquaint yourself with the think2perform team. Special thanks to office manager and company co-founder Kay May, who has worked with Doug since 1979, for arranging all the book interviews and writing time to get us to the finish line.

Oh, and one more very important acknowledgment. We thank and acknowledge you, the reader. What would a book be without our readers? Thank you!

CHAPTER ONE

Money, Health, and Happiness: How They're Connected

Happiness is not in the mere possession of money; it lies in the joy of achievement, in the thrill of creative effort.
—President Franklin D. Roosevelt

Just after 9:00 AM on September 11, 2001, life changed forever for Mary Ann Malone, though she couldn't have realized it at the time. She and her fellow Merrill Lynch traders had a disturbingly clear view of a massive fire at the World Trade Center just across the Hudson River from their Jersey City office, caused by a plane that had plowed into the WTC north tower. At 9:03 AM a second plane struck, this time crashing into the south tower. An hour later, the Merrill Lynch high-rise building was evacuated, and Mary Ann began a tortuous five-hour trip home to Westchester, just north of New York City. Major roads and bridges along her normal commute were closed, and cellular service was down, so she had no idea then that the WTC attack had taken the lives of countless friends and colleagues in the Wall Street trading community. All Mary Ann knew for certain was that she

1

desperately needed to get home to her four-year-old daughter, and that she never again wanted to work where a body of water separated her from her child. For a year afterward, Mary Ann says, "I was a mess, and my daughter had issues because I had issues."

Mary Ann had grown up in working-class Queens, New York, and dropped out of college in the fall of 1978 after only a month, because she quickly realized that the academic life was not for her. Mary Ann initially got a clerical job on a stock-trading desk. By her early twenties, Mary Ann was making a six-figure income as a NASDAQ market maker, no small feat for a woman back in the 1970s, and by the early 1990s she was undeniably wealthy. Mary Ann was financially secure, but after 9/11, she was also emotionally devastated. When Merrill Lynch offered a generous separation package in the wake of the post 9/11 financial downturn, Mary Ann jumped at the opportunity. She took her daughter to Ireland, her ancestral home, for the summer of 2002. While there, Mary Ann learned about the EDUCO seminar,[1] a powerful personal development experience. On the one-year anniversary of 9/11, Mary Ann flew to the Bahamas to attend the EDUCO seminar, and it changed her life. There, Mary Ann learned to use her mind to control her thoughts so she could live the life she wanted to live. Mary Ann discovered that she had a choice about how to live her life: She could look at life through the lens of the fear of terrorism, or she could live life through the lens of joy, positivity, and meaningful personal connections.

When Mary Ann returned from the seminar in September 2002, her friends immediately noticed a positive difference in her. She no longer focused obsessively on the past. Previously, Mary Ann had trouble talking to her friends about anything other than the awful losses of 9/11. Today, it's rare for her to think about the terror of 9/11, not because 9/11 isn't important, but because Mary Ann learned to use her mind to focus on what she can control—not the past but the future—which includes creating positive experiences for herself, her family, and her community.

Mary Ann has enjoyed taking on some exciting career challenges since then. She became a registered yoga instructor. Mary Ann also launched and operated a fitness center in Denver for four years. It was an extremely rewarding venture for Mary Ann. She loved being able

[1]EDUCO, http://www.educoworld.com/.

to help people see the benefits they would derive from the training, not just physically, but emotionally and spiritually as well. The fitness center created another priceless benefit: That was where Mary Ann met her loving partner, Tom Perkins, now 55, who had coincidentally taken the same EDUCO personal development seminar several years before Mary Ann had, and who also coincidentally became a regular client at Mary Ann's fitness center in Denver.

Sitting in Tom and Mary Ann's comfortable living room in Saint Augustine, Florida, surrounded by their two affectionate dogs, it's tempting to imagine yourself around a campfire, listening to the story of how these two very different people miraculously came together. Tom, who grew up on a Wyoming cattle ranch, got his pilot's license at age 16 and leveraged a lifelong passion for aviation into a series of lucrative aviation-support businesses; and Mary Ann, a scrappy girl from a New York outer borough, leveraged her smarts when still a teenager to become one of the earliest female stock traders on Wall Street.

Tom and Mary Ann are each strong-willed and independent. But they know how to manage occasional differences, because what joins them as a couple is a shared belief that their life is in their hands, and that they are the ultimate creators of their lives. As Mary Ann says, "The way we think is our creative tool—our gift from God, our co-creation with God." Whether you think of your source of spiritual energy as God, or Universal Energy, or Buddha, the result is the same. According to Mary Ann:

> It's not just about making money and being profitable. It's about employ-ees. It's about customers. You want not just you, but them, to flourish, thrive, and be happy. When you understand how your mind operates, you can create a positive or negative story about your life. Why not make it positive?

Mary Ann and Tom consistently focus on managing their thoughts to create alignment with their day-to-day behaviors. In addition, they also recognize the connection between their thoughts and emotions and their physical well-being. When each independently decided at some point to build a blueprint for personal happiness, both Tom and Mary Ann included physical fitness as a key ingredient. In fact, that was why Mary Ann had opened the fitness center in Denver—to help people translate their positive thoughts about vitality and fitness into their daily lives. Mary Ann, now 57, talks about how her mental state fuels her physical state. A few years ago, Mary Ann found she was able to leg press 10 repetitions at a 550-pound weight. Tom's mind-over-matter moment came when he leg pressed 1,000 pounds. Both attribute these accomplishments not just to regular workouts, but to their mental focus, a perspective they believe allows them to overperform ordinary physical expectations. But for both Tom and Mary Ann, their physical strength has a more important purpose. As Mary Ann says:

Working out regularly makes all the difference. It clears your head and makes you feel better about yourself and your body. It's very easy to understand how your mind works through working out. Everybody wants to feel good. We all have that in common. Ultimately, it's not about the way you look—though working out will improve that—but about how you feel. When you work out, you feel strong, fit, energetic, and happy.

Both Mary Ann and Tom have experienced financial stress. Mary Ann had a day trading business in the late 1990s, which was financially unsuccessful. Tom suffered significant financial losses in 2008, when his company's funding bank went bankrupt. But neither of them dwell on their business losses. Both moved on quickly, and both optimistically emphasize what they learned from business challenges.

When asked what makes them happy, Mary Ann and Tom share similar perspectives.

Mary Ann sums up the source of her happiness in this way: "Happiness is knowing who I truly am so I can connect with other people and who they truly are." Tom believes he was put here to experience life and be happy. He adds, "Experiencing life makes me happy." We authors (Doug and Ryan) can't help but imagine that our late co-author, Roy Geer, would have said essentially the same—and that he would have enjoyed meeting Tom and trading stories with him.

Mary Ann and Tom exemplify the spirit of this book. Both are financially intelligent, and both continuously invest time and resources in practices that support their physical and emotional well-being. Their home is comfortable but modest (though they could easily afford a more upscale house). They take pleasure in working in their yard. (though if they chose, they could hire someone to landscape their property.) They work out at the gym. Mary Ann is a ballroom dancer.

They enjoy time with family and friends. Mary Ann and Tom have discovered their own prescription for living life in a way that integrates money, health, and happiness.

Like Mary Ann and Tom, each of us has our own unique recipe for personal well-being. Our principles and values determine what's most important to us. Our sense of well-being depends on our ability to put those principles and values into action. Later in the book, we'll discuss practical approaches for defining and achieving personal well-being. In this chapter, we want to set the table for the three most common contributors to personal well-being—financial health, physical health, and emotional health. These three elements are also the most common potential obstacles to happiness. In fact, financial health, physical health, and happiness are profoundly interconnected. It's almost impossible to have one without the help of the other two.

MONEY AND HAPPINESS

The saying "money can't buy happiness" is a common expression, and like many sayings, it's not quite true. Research on the relationship between money and happiness is a mixed bag. For instance, psychologist and happiness researcher Sonja Lyubomirsky has found that there is a significant correlation between income and happiness, though the relationship is not as strong as we might expect.[2] Some studies suggest the relationship between money and happiness may only apply to certain types of happiness:

> When people are asked to consider how happy or satisfied they are in general, those with more money report being more happy and satisfied. But when people are asked how happy they are moment to moment in their daily lives—e.g., "How joyful, stressed, angry, affectionate, and sad were you yesterday?"—then those with more money are hardly more likely to have experienced happy feelings.[3,4]

[2] Sonja Lyubomirsky, *The Myths of Happiness: What Should Make You Happy but Doesn't. What Shouldn't Make You Happy but Does.* New York: Penguin, 2014.
[3] Kahneman, D., & Deaton, A. (2010). "High Income Improves Evaluation of Life but Not Emotional Well-Being," *PNAS*, 107, 16489–93.
[4] Luhmann, M., Schimmack, U., & Eid, M. (2011). "Stability and Variability in the Relationship between Subjective Well-Being and Income," *Journal of Research in Personality*, 45, 186–97.

How Much Is Enough?

Jamie Hale summarizes key research on the relationship between U.S. income and happiness:

> *Americans who earn $50,000 per year are much happier than those who earn $10,000 per year, but Americans who earn $5 million per year are not much happier than those who earn $100,000 per year. People who live in poor nations are much less happy than people who live in moderately wealthy nations, but people who live in moderately wealthy nations are not much less happy than people who live in extremely wealthy nations (Gilbert, 2007, p. 239).*[5]

When it comes to the relationship between annual household income and happiness, a daily survey of 1,000 U.S. residents found that self-reports of day-to-day happiness increase up to an annual household income of $75,000. After that, people don't report higher levels of day-to-day contentment.[6]

But interpreting that result is a little complicated. The study authors, psychologist Daniel Kahneman and economist Angus Deaton, differentiate between two different aspects of happiness:

• **Emotional Well-Being:** The frequency and intensity of experiences of joy, stress, sadness, anger, and affection that make one's daily life pleasant or unpleasant
• **Evaluation of Life:** How satisfied an individual is with life as a whole

Turns out that emotional well-being does tend to max out at the $75,000 number. However, when it comes to overall evaluation of one's life, people with incomes above $75,000 do feel they have a better life than do those with incomes below $75,000. Another complicating factor is that $75,000 doesn't go as far in some parts of the country as others, especially if your household is larger than the average

[5] Jamie Hale, M.S. "What Makes Us Happy?" Psych Central, https://psychcentral.com/lib/what-makes-us-happy/.
[6] Daniel Kahneman and Angus Deaton, "High Income Improves Evaluation of Life but Not Emotional Well-Being," *Proceedings of the National Academy of Sciences of the United States of America*, 2010. Accessed at: http://www.pnas.org/content/107/38/16489. Retrieved June 1, 2017.

2.9 members the study assumes. Advisor Perspectives calculated a state-by-state cost-of-living adjustment to the $75K "Happiness Benchmark" from the Kahneman-Deaton study.[7] (See Figure 1.1.)

FIGURE 1.1   COLA HAPPINESS BENCHMARK INCOMES BY STATE

The Cost-of-Living Adjusted "Happiness Benchmark"
for the 50 States and DC in 2015

The Deaton-Kahneman $75K Happiness Benchmark adjusted for the average cost of living; based on data from the Council for Community & Economic Research. Values are rounded to the closest $100.

$107,000

$75,000 Happiness Benchmark

$61,600

The $75K Happiness Benchmark: Cost-of-Living Adjusted by State (and DC)					
Mississippi	$61,600	North Carolina	$68,500	**National Average**	**$75,000**
Kentucky	$63,600	South Carolina	$68,800	Illinois	$76,000
Arkansas	$64,400	South Dakota	$69,000	Pennsylvania	$76,500
Alabama	$64,900	Texas	$69,100	Oregon	$77,400
Tennessee	$65,000	Utah	$69,500	Washington	$77,800
Oklahoma	$65,400	Wisconsin	$69,800	Maryland	$81,800
Idaho	$65,700	Montana	$70,500	Maine	$83,000
Indiana	$65,900	New Mexico	$71,100	Vermont	$84,400
Ohio	$66,400	North Dakota	$71,300	New Jersey	$85,200
Michigan	$66,700	Minnesota	$71,400	New Hampshire	$85,700
Missouri	$66,900	Florida	$71,700	Rhode Island	$86,700
Iowa	$67,100	Wyoming	$72,900	Massachusetts	$90,300
West Virginia	$67,300	Virginia	$73,000	Alaska	$91,900
Louisiana	$67,500	Arizona	$73,400	Connecticut	$92,200
Nebraska	$67,900	Delaware	$73,400	California	$94,800
Kansas	$67,900	Colorado	$74,100	District of Columbia	$99,000
Georgia	$68,000	Nevada	$74,400	New York	$100,800
				Hawaii	$107,000

Source: Advisor Perspectives

[7]Doug Short, "Happiness Revisited: A Household Income of $75K?" Advisor Perspectives, 2016, https://www.advisorperspectives.com/dshort/commentaries/2016/10/21/happiness-revisited-a-household-income-of-75K. Retrieved June 1, 2017.

For example, in Mississippi, $61K will buy you as much happiness as $100K will give you in the state of New York.

This study echoes many others, which show that people who are in financial survival mode experience a great deal of stress. However, when they are able to earn enough to feel financially stable, additional income doesn't have much impact on day-to-day happiness. Once someone reaches the set happiness income level for their geographic area—they appear to be just about as happy as someone who is making a million dollars a year or more. In fact, there is some research that indicates high-income people may be less happy than moderate earners, possibly because the lifestyle that high-net-worth individuals adopt often makes it more difficult to enjoy life's simpler pleasures.

National Geographic Fellow Dan Buettner, in his book, *Thrive: Finding Happiness the Blue Zones Way*, asked a number of happiness experts if money can buy happiness. Ed Diener says yes, though he notes some important exceptions. That's because money means different things to different people. Studies show that materialistic people are rarely happy because they want more than they can have. According to Diener, "It is generally good for your happiness to *have* money, but toxic to your happiness to *want* money too much."[8]

Financial Stress

Though having more money may not buy more happiness, having too little money almost always causes stress that's detrimental to happiness. It's interesting to note that the $50,000-a-year income (which research indicates is a minimum amount that provides the ability to pay one's bills) is not much lower than the median family income in the United States. That would suggest that nearly half of U.S. families don't have incomes that allow them to meet their basic financial needs, and therefore are likely to experience varying degrees of financial stress. Research also shows that the lower one's income, the higher the level of financial stress. Other studies support the idea that financial stress is widespread.

[8] Quoted in Dan Buettner, *Thrive: Finding Happiness the Blue Zones Way* (Washington, D.C.: National Geographic Society, 2011), p. 16.

A series of annual surveys conducted by the American Psychological Association[9] confirms that money remains the top life stressor among Americans. APA's 2015 survey found that for the majority of Americans (64 percent), money is a "somewhat" or "very significant" source of stress. Responses to their 2015 survey showed that nearly three-quarters of Americans report feeling stressed about money at some point in the previous month, with nearly a quarter reporting that they experienced extreme stress in the prior month. The APA survey also found differences in levels of financial stress in different demographic groups, with women, parents, younger people, and members of lower income families all reporting the highest levels of stress. For example, 77 percent of parents, 75 percent of Millennials, and 76 percent of Gen Xers reported experiencing financial stress.

The 2017 PwC Employee Financial Wellness Survey[10] found similar results. In the PwC survey, finance was the top cause of stress for all employee age groups—Millennials, Gen X, and Boomers alike. Overall, 53 percent of employees reported that dealing with their financial situation was stressful; 45 percent of employees said that financial matters caused them the most life stress—about as much as other life stressors such as job, health, or relationships combined. For Millennials, financial burdens may be even greater. Of the 40 percent of Millennial employees who have student loans, a whopping 83 percent say they are stressed about their finances. What's more, financial stress may be getting worse over time—in the 2017 PwC survey, 47 percent of employees said that their stress had increased during the previous 12 months.

Surprisingly, financial stress is not just a function of limited income or assets. According to the 2017 PwC survey, cash and debt issues are an increasing concern even for employees earning $100,000 or more. For example, nearly 60 percent of high income earners regularly carry credit card balances. It's common for people with net worth above $1 million to experience financial stress. No matter how healthy your investment accounts, you may understandably worry about running out of

[9] Sophie Bethune, "Money Stress Weighs on Americans' Health," American Psychological Association, 2015, Vol. 46, No. 4, print version: page 38, http://www.apa.org/monitor/2015/04/money-stress.aspx, retrieved February 13, 2017.
[10] "2017 Employee Financial Wellness Survey," PwC, April 2017, https://www.pwc.com/us/en/private-company-services/publications/financial-well-being-retirement-survey.html, retrieved July 28, 2017.

money. Co-author Doug's father, who passed away just before turning 85, was in very good financial shape and still worried about money. Even ultra-high-net-worth individuals (UHNWIs), that is, those with assets exceeding $30 million, may suffer considerable stress. As financial professional and writer Greg DePersio points out:

> *Many argue the financial problems plaguing UHNWIs are ones most of the world would love to have, kind of like being too good-looking, too smart, or having too many dates to choose from on a Saturday night. These challenges include changing tax codes, estate planning, sustaining their lifestyles during retirement, and protecting their current levels of wealth. While it may sound crazy to someone working an average job for average pay, a UHNWI worth $50 million is often scared to death of descending to simple millionaire status.*[11]

According to DePersio, their worry is not without cause. They may be highly paid CEOs who fear the loss of salary if they lose their job or retire. Also, UHNWIs often accumulate their wealth from high-risk investments, and may legitimately fear heavy losses in the event of a recession or stock market crash. Finally, many UHNWIs don't manage their money well, leading to significant losses.

Not Enough

We know that financial stress is rampant. But how does financial stress affect our lives? It won't surprise you that money issues and financial stress have a profound impact on personal and family well-being and stability. For example, as family therapist John Dakin and psychologist Richard Wampler found:

> *Conflict about finances ranks among the top reasons contributing to divorce (Lawrence, Thomasson, Wozniak, & Prawitz, 1993). "…[C]ouples dissatisfied with their financial situation frequently consider their entire relationship a failure" (Blumstein & Schwarz, 1983, p. 55)*[12]

[11] Greg DePersio, "The Worst Financial Problems Ultra-High-Net-Worth-Individuals (UHNWIs) Face," *Investopedia*, 2015, http://www.investopedia.com/articles/personal-finance/111915/worst-financial-problems-ultrahighnetworthindividuals-uhnwis-face.asp. Retrieved June 1, 2017.
[12] John Dakin and Richard Wampler, "Money Doesn't Buy Happiness, but It Helps: Marital Satisfaction, Psychological Distress, and Demographic Differences Between Low- and Middle-Income Clinic Couples," *The American Journal of Family Therapy*, 36:300–311, 2008.

And because lower-income couples are more likely to deal with high levels of financial stress, they have a higher divorce rate than that of middle- or upper-income couples.[13]

Debt and Depression

For most people struggling with financial challenges, being in debt plays a major role in their experience of financial stress. John Gathergood, an economist at the University of Nottingham, conducted research that demonstrated that people who have difficulty paying off debts are more than twice as likely as others to experience mental health problems such as depression and severe anxiety. Analyses of numerous research studies confirm that the higher the amount of debt, the more severe the symptoms of depression and anxiety.[14] People carry debt for various reasons: some because of poor financial habits, or because household and medical costs exceed their income. As the PwC study indicated, people with student loans experience the most financial stress. And given what we know about the cost of higher education, student loan debt amounts can be extremely high. Since Millennials bear the brunt of student loan debt, it's important for Millennials themselves, as well as parents, employers, and financial advisors, to pay particular attention to the potential impact of financial stress on Millennials' emotional well-being.

The relationship between finances and happiness is probably stronger than the research about annual income and financial stress can fully capture. Many people are "just one paycheck away" from financial disaster. Consider these scenarios in which you currently have a well-paying job and you comfortably make monthly payments on debts such as a mortgage, car payment, and a student loan:

- You are unexpectedly laid off from your job.
- You are diagnosed with a serious illness.
- A family member now needs 24/7 care.
- Your child has special educational needs that cannot be met in a public school.

[13] Ibid.
[14] Kristen Kuchar, "The Emotional Effects of Debt," *The Simple Dollar*, http://www.thesimpledollar.com/the-emotional-effects-of-debt.

How would you manage these changes in your life situation? Though you may have a good job, it's likely that you may not have enough savings to handle unexpected crises. In fact, a recent Bankrate.com survey showed that only 37 percent of Americans have enough savings to cover a $500 or $1,000 emergency.[15] When it comes to being prepared for financial crises, women are at even greater risk. According to the 2017 PwC Employee Financial Wellness Survey, 54 percent of women reported that they don't have enough emergency savings to cover unexpected expenses.[16] Clearly, a high percentage of people either currently experience financial stress, or are at risk of unexpected situations that would trigger significant financial stress. That's why we authors place so much importance on the relationship between financial stress and happiness. As you'll see in Chapter 4, taking steps to minimize financial stress by developing and leveraging your financial intelligence is one of the most powerful approaches you can use to enhance your life satisfaction. Several years ago, co-authors Doug and Ryan met with Helen Riess, Associate Professor of Psychiatry, Harvard Medical School and co-founder of Empathetics, Inc., to discuss her findings on the relationship between finances and overall well-being. Riess confirmed, "When it comes to happiness the most basic fundamentals are related to physical health, relationship health, and financial health. If you can take steps to reduce financial stress, that will definitely favorably impact your physical health and therefore your happiness."[17]

MONEY AND HEALTH

So far we've focused on the intersection between finances and happiness. In this section we'll concentrate on the intersection between money and health.

---

[15] Maggie McGrath, "63% of Americans Don't Have Enough Savings to Cover a $500 Emergency," *Forbes*, January 6, 2016, https://www.forbes.com/sites/maggiemcgrath/2016/01/06/63-of-americans-dont-have-enough-savings-to-cover-a-500-emergency/#507f71bb4e0d.

[16] "2017 Employee Financial Wellness Survey," *PwC*, April 2017, https://www.pwc.com/us/en/private-company-services/publications/financial-well-being-retirement-survey.html, retrieved July 28, 2017.

[17] Conversation between Dr. Helen Riess, Doug Lennick, and Ryan Goulart, August 7, 2014.

Not Enough Income; Not Enough Health

Income and health have always been interrelated. Sandro Galea, dean of the Boston University School of Public Health, points out that as far back as 1841, pioneering British epidemiologist William Farr discovered that death rates in English asylums were highest among poor patients.[18] Fast forwarding to the present day, a 2016 UNICEF report, "The State of the World's Children 2016: A fair chance for every child,"[19] presents disturbing statistics on the relationship between income and child and maternal health:

> *In terms of child survival, while the absolute gap has substantially narrowed since 1990, great inequities remain between rich and poor countries. The relative child mortality gap between sub-Saharan Africa and South Asia on one side and high-income countries on the other has barely changed in a quarter of a century. Children born in sub-Saharan Africa are 12 times more likely than their counterparts in high-income countries to die before their fifth birthday, just as they were in 1990.*

> *A child born in Sierra Leone today is about 30 times more likely to die before age 5 than a child born in the United Kingdom. Women in sub-Saharan Africa face a 1-in-36 lifetime risk of maternal mortality, compared to 1 in 3,300 in high-income countries.*

According to U.S. Centers for Disease Control (CDC) research, poor adults (annual incomes less than $35,000) are about five times more likely to report they are in fair or poor health than adults earning $100,000 or more. Low-income adults also have significantly higher rates of a wide range of diseases and health conditions.[20]

Figure 1.2 illustrates the prevalence of diseases among adults based on their income.

[18] Sandro Galea, "Income and Health, Part 1," *Boston University School of Public Health*, December 4, 2016, https://www.bu.edu/sph/2016/12/04/income-and-health-part-1/.
[19] "The State of the World's Children 2016: A Fair Chance for Every Child," *UNICEF*, June 2016, https://www.unicef.org/publications/files/UNICEF_SOWC_2016.pdf.
[20] Summary Health Statistics for the U.S. Population: National Health Interview Survey, 2011, U.S. Department of Health and Human Services, Centers for Disease Control and Prevention, Series 10, Number 255, December 2011, https://www.cdc.gov/nchs/data/series/sr_10/sr10_255.pdf.

FIGURE **1.2**   **INCIDENCE OF DISEASE RELATED TO INCOME**

DISEASE OR ILLNESS	ANNUAL FAMILY INCOME				
	Less than $35,000	$35,000-49,999	$50,000-74,999	$75,000-99,999	$100,000 or more
Coronary heart disease	8.1	6.5	6.3	5.3	4.9
Stroke	3.9	2.5	2.3	1.8	1.6
Emphysema	3.2	2.5	1.4	1.0	0.8
Chronic bronchitis	6.3	4.0	4.4	2.2	2.4
Diabetes	11.0	10.4	8.3	5.6	5.9
Ulcers	8.7	6.7	6.5	4.7	4.4
Kidney disease	3.0	1.9	1.3	0.9	0.9
Liver disease	2.0	1.6	1.0	0.6	0.7
Chronic arthritis	33.4	30.3	27.9	27.4	24.4
Hearing trouble	17.2	16.0	16.0	16.2	12.4
Vision trouble	12.7	9.8	7.5	5.7	6.6
No teeth	11.6	7.8	5.5	4.2	4.1

Source: U.S. Centers for Disease Control

There are a number of reasons why low-income individuals suffer poorer health than others. In some instances, lack of financial resources may limit access to healthcare. For example, 28 percent of those who responded to PwC's Employee Financial Wellness Survey said that financial issues have affected their health. APA's Stress in America: Paying with Our Health survey[21] revealed that nearly one in five Americans either skipped or considered skipping a necessary visit for medical treatment because of financial constraints.

The relationship between low income and health isn't simply a matter of inability to pay for health services. The impact of financial

[21] Sophie Bethune, "Money Stress Weighs on Americans' Health," American Psychological Association, 2015, Vol 46, No. 4, print version: page 38, http://www.apa.org/monitor/2015/04/money-stress.aspx.

stress itself is a major contributor to health problems. One study on the negative effects of financial stress on physical well-being comes from Laura Choi of the Federal Bank of San Francisco.[22] Among her key findings:

- When people are dealing with significant debt, they are much more likely to report health problems.
- The threat of ongoing debt or insufficient income can result in feelings of loss of control, anxiety, and other mental and emotional stress.
- Chronic financial stress has been linked to a cycle of increased workplace absenteeism, diminished workplace performance, and depression.

According to a paper in *The Journal of the American Osteopathic Association*, between 75 and 90 percent of visits to primary care providers are for stress-related issues. Arta Bakshandeh, senior medical officer with Alignment Healthcare in Los Angeles, highlights the relationship of stress to health when he says, "Of the patients that I would attribute their medical problems to stress, the overwhelming majority have money at the root.... Most commonly, these patients complain of headaches, elevated blood pressure, ulcers, depression, and moderate to severe anxiety." Since financial stress is the most common type of stress, in effect, it's likely that a majority of primary care patients are seeing their care providers for conditions related to financial stress.

Financial stress can contribute to a host of physical conditions, including heart disease, gastrointestinal problems, weight issues, diabetes, and high blood pressure. Another potential impact of financial stress may be seen in the growing prevalence of substance abuse. The U.S. "opioid epidemic" is now receiving long-overdue attention as a serious issue. However, most media reports provide superficial explanations for the crisis, tending to attribute the root of the problem to excessive prescribing of opioid drugs for pain. Most political responses

[22] "Laura Choi, "Financial Stress and Its Physical Effects on Individuals and Communities," *Federal Reserve Bank of San Francisco Community Development Investment Review*, December 2009, https://core.ac.uk/download/pdf/6223933.pdf.

center around legislation restricting legal access to opioids in various ways. Not enough attention has been paid to the fact that the opioid epidemic seems to be most acute in certain parts of the United States, such as the "Rust Belt," where manufacturing and coal industry jobs have been decimated over several decades, and where unemployment and underemployment is high. Bloomberg is among the few media outlets that report on the connection between this tragic social issue and economics.[23] We believe that a major contributor to the opioid crisis is financial stress caused by job loss and lack of job opportunities in economically depressed regions. Dealing with such severe financial insecurity is likely to cause a host of health conditions and emotional issues that may lead people to seek out pain medication, whether from qualified medical professionals or illegal sources.

How Financial Resources Support Health

Now let's turn to the upside of the money–health relationship. One clear connection is that having a certain amount of money gives us access to resources that promote health, for example, high-quality food, access to better healthcare, ability to live in safer neighborhoods, and access to fitness resources such as expensive sports equipment and gym memberships. Most of us recognize that financial health and physical health can and ideally should be related. For example, according to a survey conducted by TD Bank in 2015, 70 percent of Americans believe that being in good shape financially can have a positive impact on overall health and well-being. This number increases to 80 percent among those who have a financial plan.[24,25] A report by UK-based global financial services company Aviva reinforces the link between financial

---

[23]Noah Smith, "Another Reason to Fight Opioid Addiction: Economics," *Bloomberg.com*, March 3, 2017, https://www.bloomberg.com/view/articles/2017-03-03/another-reason-to-fight-opioid-addiction-economics.
[24]TD Bank Fiscal Fit Survey, 2015, http://tdfiscalfitness.com/.
[25]"Financial and Physical Well-Being Go Hand-in-Hand for a Majority of Americans, New Survey Finds," TD Bank, January 26, 2015, https://mediaroom.tdbank.com/2015-01-26-Financial-and-Physical-Well-Being-Go-Hand-in-Hand-for-a-Majority-of-Americans-New-Survey-Finds.

planning and happiness. According to Guardian's Rebecca Smithers, the Aviva study reveals:

> . . . *overall happiness, well-being, and self-esteem are influenced by our sense of financial control and not by how much we lodge in the bank every month . . .*
>
> . . . *those with sensible financial plans in place are happier overall and have a stronger sense of "financial wellbeing," regardless of their pay packet.*[26]

What accounts for this belief? Most people say that when their finances are in good shape—and they have a financial plan—it's much easier to achieve goals for fitness and health.

When it comes to Americans' current fiscal and physical health status, only about one-third of respondents (36 percent) said they are satisfied with their current financial health. Yet among those who are satisfied with their physical health, 65 percent said they are also satisfied with their financial health.

"It's no surprise that getting your finances in order can relieve stress, but our research shows that it can also positively affect physical fitness," said Ryan Bailey, head of Retail Deposit Products, TD Bank. "With [New Year's] resolutions still top of mind, it's important for Americans to know that working on your wallet can also benefit your waistline. You don't have to choose one or the other."[27]

Erin Livermore and her husband, Doug, suffered sticker shock when they first moved with their two young girls to the pricey Washington, D.C., area after 10 years living in several different parts of the country where cost of living was fairly low. Though they both found good professional jobs, housing and childcare costs left them in a precarious financial state, barely covering basic expenses each month. Erin felt oppressed and stressed. Then after a year at her job as an accountant with a major media company, she landed a promotion to

[26] Rebecca Smithers, "Happiness Linked to Financial Planning, Research Shows," *The Guardian*, June 16, 2010, https://www.theguardian.com/money/2010/jun/16/happiness-financial-planning-aviva.

[27] As quoted in "Financial and Physical Well-Being Go Hand-in-Hand for a Majority of Americans, New Survey Finds," TD Bank, January 26, 2015, https://mediaroom.tdbank.com/2015-01-26-Financial-and-Physical-Well-Being-Go-Hand-in-Hand-for-a-Majority-of-Americans-New-Survey-Finds.

senior accountant, with a modest salary increase. But it was enough to give her a little leftover money to pay for some exercise classes. Those classes helped her in many ways: She gained physical strength, lost weight, and felt better about herself. Though Erin was getting up an hour earlier many mornings to go to her fitness class, she began to experience more sustained energy and focus during the day. Erin believes that her fitness program increased her productivity at work, and actually helped set the stage for a rapid second promotion to assistant controller. Erin promptly signed up for some additional exercise classes she hadn't been able to afford before.

Health Practices Can Improve Your Finances

As mentioned, you can improve your health by leveraging money to access health-promoting resources, including medical care, fitness activities, and high-quality foods and nutritional supplements. But the reverse is also true: Adopting health-promoting practices can result in financial gains. For example, seemingly minor actions intended to improve physical health have also been found to have positive effects on financial well-being. For example:

- A full night's sleep has been linked to a 5 percent increase in pay.[28]
- Regular exercise is related to a 7 to 12 percent increase in pay.[29]

How do health-promoting practices translate into such financial gains? One example: Employees in midlife who get involved in fitness activities become more productive on the job. Since they tend to continue fitness practices after retirement, they place less of a burden on retiree healthcare programs. Therefore, forward-looking companies who provide physical activity programs or fitness centers encourage the kind of physical fitness behaviors that result in lower employee and retiree costs down the road.

[28] Brett Arends, "A Full Night's Sleep Can Really Pay Off—in Salary and Investments," *Wall Street Journal*, September 18, 2014, https://www.wsj.com/articles/a-full-nights-sleep-can-really-pay-offin-salary-and-investments-1411056919.
[29] Victor Lipman, "New Study Links Exercise to Higher Pay," *Forbes*, June 8, 2012, https://www.forbes.com/sites/victorlipman/2012/06/08/new-study-links-exercise-to-higher-pay/#697b4c405db6.

HAPPINESS AND HEALTH

In recent years, there has been a wealth of research trying to identify the link between emotions and health. One of the most significant studies, one being conducted by Harvard's School of Public Health, seeks to answer these questions:[30]

- Could a sunny outlook mean fewer colds and less heart disease?
- Do hope and curiosity somehow protect against hypertension, diabetes, and respiratory tract infections?
- Do happier people live longer—and, if so, why?

Common sense tells us that negative emotions lead to unhappiness. But what are the emotions and personal characteristics that can positively influence our health? Social psychologist Laura Kubzansky, Lee Kum Kee Professor of Social and Behavioral Sciences at the Harvard School of Public Health, is part of the HSPH research trying to understand how positive emotions influence health. In a large study that followed adults across their life span for 20 years, Kubzansky found that "emotional vitality" (which she defined as a sense of enthusiasm, hopefulness, engagement in life, and ability to face stresses) reduced the risk of coronary heart disease. Figure 1.3 summarizes the research on certain happiness-related attributes that the Harvard School of Public Health study and elsewhere have identified as promoting positive health outcomes.

Other research demonstrates the impact of happiness on health. Happiness is heart-protective. Middle-aged men and women who rated themselves as being happy over the course of a working day received a variety of laboratory test results that are associated with lower risk of heart disease. Happiness has also been shown to reduce the risk of viral illness, suggesting that happiness has a beneficial effect on our immune systems. So there's clear evidence that health and happiness are related, but does one cause the other? It's easy to imagine that being healthy leads to feelings of happiness. But can the mere fact of being happy improve your health? The answer is probably yes. There is some

[30] Sara Rimer and Madeline Drexler, "Happiness and Health: The Biology of Emotion—and What It May Teach Us about Helping People to Live Longer." Harvard T.H. Chan School of Public Health (2011), https://www.hsph.harvard.edu/news/magazine/happiness-stress-heart-disease.

FIGURE 1.3   KEYS TO A HAPPIER, HEALTHIER LIFE

Keys to a happier, healthier life

Research suggests that certain personal attributes—whether inborn or shaped by positive life circumstances—help some people avoid or healthfully manage diseases such as heart attacks, strokes, diabetes, and depression. These include:

- Emotional vitality: a sense of enthusiasm, hopefulness, engagement

- Optimism: the perspective that good things will happen, and that one's actions account for the good things that occur in life

- Supportive networks of family and friends

- Being good at "self-regulation," i.e. bouncing back from stressful challenges and knowing that things will eventually look up again; choosing healthy behaviors such as physical activity and eating well; and avoiding risky behaviors such as unsafe sex, drinking alcohol to excess, and regular overeating

---

Source: Laura Kubzansky, Harvard T.H. Chan School of Public Health

intriguing research suggesting that maintaining a happy mood can have positive health effects later in life; that is, happiness can prevent future disease. Take, for example, results of a large, long-term Canadian study of heart disease:[31]

> . . . *researchers invited nearly 2,000 Canadians into the lab to talk about their anger and stress at work. Observers rated them on a scale of one to five for the extent to which they expressed positive emotions like joy, happiness, excitement, enthusiasm, and contentment. Ten years later, the researchers checked in with the participants to see how they were doing—and it turned out that the happier ones were less likely to have developed coronary heart disease. In fact, for each one-point increase in positive emotions they had expressed, their heart disease risk was 22 percent lower.*

Based on these results, the researchers concluded that heart disease risk could be dramatically lowered by working with people to treat any depression and by helping people increase their level of positive emotions. And as you'll discover later in the book, there are many direct and practical ways to increase your level of happiness.

[31] Karina W. Davidson, Elizabeth Mostofsky, and William Whang, "Don't Worry, Be Happy: Positive Affect and Reduced 10-Year Incident Coronary Heart Disease: The Canadian Nova Scotia Health Survey," *European Heart Journal*, 2010 May; 31(9): 1065–1070.

* * * * * *

By studying the research and through years of experience in coaching individuals to improve their business and personal performance, we co-authors have developed effective tools to help you leverage the intersection of money, health, and happiness in positive ways. Co-author Doug developed a model (the alignment model) and a set of practices that have brought him and many others a great deal of life satisfaction. Following the alignment model doesn't mean you'll always be 100% happy. There are times when the intersection of money, health, and happiness can become a vicious circle. There are life events you can't control that can trigger a downturn in your well-being, and make it more difficult to follow the steps that sustain your well-being. But even during dark times, there are practices we'll share that can keep you from hitting rock bottom and restore your sense of well-being much more quickly than otherwise.

As financial advisors, leaders, and business coaches, we have been fortunate to inspire thousands of people to live their best lives at the intersection of money, health, and happiness. Our aim in this book is to help you do the same.

Living in Alignment

Happiness is when what you think, what you say, and what you do are in harmony.

—Mahatma Gandhi

It was 5:30 AM on a wintry Boston morning. Fifty seven-year-old Eileen Kelly* hit the top of her alarm clock, feeling an instant rush of dread. Fifteen minutes later, stepping out of the shower, she glanced at her reflection in the bathroom mirror and grimaced at the bags under her eyes. "I'm really getting old," she thought. Eileen was tired of the daily grind: Shake off her sluggishness and get herself out the door on time. Deal with the stress of a rush-hour commute. Manage the demands of a long day as a nurse anesthetist[1] at an outpatient surgery center. Drive home, heat up a frozen dinner, drink a glass of wine—sometimes two or three. Watch TV, brush her teeth. Then lights out on another lackluster day.

Eileen's life hadn't always felt like this. She used to enjoy the challenges of her job and the camaraderie of the surgery center.

---

*Eileen Kelly is a composite persona based on our interviews with several individuals who have completed the process of learning to live in alignment.

[1] Studies place nurse anesthetists near the top of the ranks of most-stressful jobs, though average annual salary is favorable at $147,256, http://career-profiles.careertrends.com/stories/10430/most-stressful-jobs#22-Nurse-Anesthetist. Retrieved April 2, 2017.

But over the last few years, work that had once seemed invigorating now seemed routine and boring. Work friends were beginning to retire, and she didn't have much in common with the young professionals who were replacing them.

Eileen also used to enjoy going out with friends to plays and concerts, but since her divorce a few years ago, Eileen noticed she was being left out of gatherings with her married friends. Other friends had retired and relocated to warmer climes. Eileen loved spending time with her son and his family, but she didn't get to see them very often since he'd taken a job on the West Coast. As if that wasn't hard enough, Eileen's dog, Daisy, had recently died, and she found it hard to keep up her regular neighborhood walks without her faithful companion by her side.

Feeling lonely, Eileen tried joining a women's group at her church and a book club, but their members seemed to have their own cliques, so after a while she gave up on trying to socialize, and settled into a more solitary routine. Eileen discovered that she enjoyed collecting—mostly vintage dishes, glassware, and silverware that reminded her of her grandmother's house growing up. She started scouring weekend yard sales and flea markets in search of treasures. Eileen also spent increasing amounts of time watching shopping channels. She enjoyed the banter of the people selling products and their chatty conversations with happy customers. Eileen finally felt part of a community—the TV shopping community. Before long, Eileen was buying clothing and jewelry from QVC and HSN several times a week, dipping into her savings account to cover her compulsive spending.

Then one morning, Eileen woke up to a different kind of alarm. Breathless, nauseous, and suffering abdominal pain, Eileen called 911, and was rushed to the hospital. Fortunately, Eileen had not had a heart attack, but she was at high risk for one. She was diagnosed with pancreatitis and Type 2 diabetes, either of which can be life threatening. Her medical history and lab work provided some clues about her "sudden" illness. It turned out that in the last year, Eileen had gained 20 pounds and her blood pressure had become quite high. Her blood glucose level, a marker for diabetes, was also very high. In one year, Eileen's cholesterol level had jumped from normal to high. Her liver enzymes were abnormal, suggesting she might be drinking too much alcohol, or at a minimum, that her weight gain had led to a dangerous condition called "fatty liver." Eileen's primary care doctor visited her the night before she was released from the hospital. She reviewed Eileen's chart, pulled up a chair beside her patient's bed, and gently asked, "Eileen, what's going on with you?" "I don't know," Eileen said, tearing up. "All I know is I hate waking up in the morning."

THE ALIGNMENT MODEL

In a few short years, Eileen had lost a lot—her marriage, social connections, enthusiasm for work, savings—and now her health. Eileen no doubt valued family, fitness, social relationships, financial security, and interesting, well-paying work. But because Eileen lost the will to act consistently with those values, she allowed herself to become victim to a vicious cycle of misfortunes. For Eileen, the intersection of money, health, and happiness had become a crash scene. Landing in the hospital was quite a wake-up call. She knew bad health was just one of her problems. Eileen decided she would do whatever it took to get her life back. Eileen felt overwhelmed, so at her doctor's suggestion, she began to work with a life coach who taught her an approach called the "alignment model."

Your Life in Three Frames

If you want to maintain or improve your life satisfaction, it's useful to align who you really are with who you would like to be ideally. When you're in alignment, you feel good—you're happier, healthier, and more financially fit. So begin by visualizing your life in three frames: your *ideal self* (including your principles, values, and beliefs), your *goals* (including your purpose, goals, and wants), and your *behavior* (including your thoughts, emotions, and actions.).

Together, these three frames represent the alignment model (Figure 2.1). Alignment happens when each frame is consistent with the others. You are in alignment when the way you behave is consistent with the goals you've set for your life, and when the goals you've set are consistent with what you value most for your life. The power of the alignment model is that it will help you make the best possible life choices and achieve the greatest satisfaction in all dimensions of your life. Eileen took an important step toward living in

FIGURE 2.1   ALIGNMENT MODEL

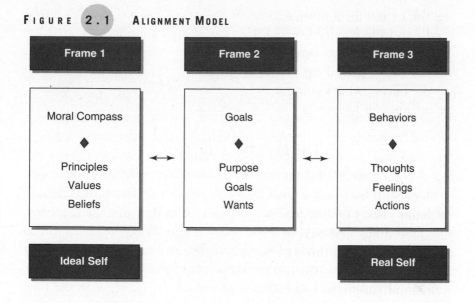

alignment when she acknowledged that she needed help and made the commitment to work with a coach to identify her life goals and act to achieve them.

Living in alignment is an ideal. It represents the person we would like to be at our best. Living in alignment may sometimes be difficult, but it doesn't require superhuman acts. It is about the day-to day steps we take to do what's needed to reach our goals. Living in alignment is also not accidental. It requires doing things on purpose and for a purpose. Living in alignment is a two-part process. First, you build your own personal alignment model by understanding what's inside of these three frames:

- **Ideal Self**—Moral Compass: What are your most important principles and values?
- **Goals**—What do you want to accomplish, personally and professionally?
- **Real Self**—Behavior: What decisions will you make and what concrete actions will you take to achieve your goals? (thoughts, emotions, actions)

Then, once you've built your own alignment model and know what should be in each frame, you work consciously and consistently to maintain alignment among your frames—simple, but as you might already suspect, far from easy.

IDEAL SELF

Your ideal self includes the core moral principles and values that are the foundation of who you would ideally like to be as a productive and fulfilled human being. Principles and values overlap. Principles are fundamental beliefs that have been embedded in human society for so long that they are now widely recognized as universal. Values, on the other hand, tend to be an expression of what's important to us individually. The values that matter most to you can be quite different from the values that matter most to someone else.

In Doug's previous book, *Moral Intelligence,* he and co-author Fred Kiel surveyed the research on universal principles and identified four primary principles held in common globally:

* Integrity
* Responsibility
* Compassion
* Forgiveness

What do these principles really mean in practice? We follow these principles with the help of several moral competencies, or skills, that define each principle.

> Integrity means: *acting consistently with principles, values, and beliefs, telling the truth, standing up for what is right,* and *keeping promises.*
> Responsibility includes: *taking responsibility for personal choices, admitting mistakes and failures, and embracing responsibility for serving others.*
> The essence of Compassion is *actively caring about others.*
> Finally, we demonstrate Forgiveness by *letting go of one's own mistakes, and letting go of others' mistakes.*

It's no coincidence that people who enjoy high levels of financial, physical, and emotional well-being all seem to place high importance on living in alignment with principles. They listen carefully to the call of moral principles that already lie within all of us.

RESPONSIBILITY

All four principles—integrity, responsibility, compassion, and forgiveness—are important, but the principle of responsibility is key to overall well-being. Here is a secret that the happiest people have discovered. Responsibility is their guiding principle. They know that they are in charge. They know it's up to them to make sound decisions about finances, health, and overall well-being. For example, each of us is completely responsible for our financial well-being. This doesn't mean that each of us is responsible for becoming wealthy. But we are responsible for becoming financially independent, that is, not dependent on others for our financial health. We may never earn enough money so that work becomes optional, but we are responsible for making plans and choices that allow us to thrive, regardless of how much or little money we have. Consider this example of financial responsibility: Gallup polling conducted at the end of 2008 during a historic recession found that while only 36 percent of all Americans at the time felt that they were "thriving," almost 30 percent of the poorest Americans, those living on less than $24,000 a year, also described themselves as "thriving." According to Gallup at the time, "While the lowest-income Americans are still those most likely to be struggling, they did not see the stark increase in struggling in the first two weeks of November [2008] that those making over $24,000 did." What explains the difference between people who, despite their low incomes, still felt that they were thriving, while so many people earning three to four times as much reported that they were struggling? Fortunately we haven't had another recession since then, but if this was true during a period of great economic turmoil, it's probably just as true now. Clearly, it's not about how much you earn. It is about your attitude about your life.

Responsibility is also key to our physical well-being. Though we don't have complete control over the state of our health, we are responsible for the choices we make that affect our health. For most diseases, lifestyle choices are far more important than genetics in determining whether we develop that disease. As an example, recent research shows that even people with a high inherited risk of heart disease can cut that risk by more than half by exercising, losing weight, and quitting smoking.[2]

[2]As reported by Dennis Thompson, "Healthy Lifestyle Can Overcome Genetic Risk for Heart Disease," 2016, http://www.upi.com/Health_News/2016/11/13/Healthy-lifestyle-can-overcome-genetic-risk-for-heart-disease/4971479085350/. Retrieved March 30, 2017.

Finally, we are responsible for our overall sense of personal well-being. As emphasized in the previous chapter, happiness is not something that just happens to us. We can and should take actions to increase our happiness, no matter what our external circumstances are.

DOUG'S STORY

I got a promotion in 1983 that came fully equipped with a $100,000 pay cut. I had not fully paid off my 1982 taxes, but needed money to invest in my new business opportunity, so I made a poor decision not to pay my taxes on time. Instead I used my money to get launched. Among other expenses, my new job required that I furnish the office. At the same time, I was transitioning from working as an independent contractor to becoming a W2 employee, so I was making less money and my cash flow was worse. To complicate the situation further, I owed monthly child support payments which were based on my previous income. I made a point never to miss those payments, no matter how much I had to scrimp. But my own household suffered. And I still owed back taxes. I thought I had a payment arrangement with the IRS, but I found out later I was mistaken. One evening I came home to my beautiful pregnant wife, Beth Ann, and a dark house. The electricity and water had been shut off. The IRS had garnished my wages. I wasn't getting any paychecks. And I had no immediate way to pay our bills. That's when I knew that happiness is a state of mind, not a state of affairs—because my circumstances were miserable, but I wasn't miserable. It might have been tempting to jump out a second-story window. Instead, I maintained a sense of well-being while I worked to dig us out of a financial mess. I believe my ability to stay happy when things were difficult helped me get our family back on a firm financial footing as quickly as possible.

VALUES

Though values are personal beliefs about what is important to us as individuals, values are usually consistent with principles, and they allow us to put our own stamp on the meaning of the principles. For example, responsibility is a key principle, but our values help us choose how we individually express the principle of responsibility. We may value competence, challenge, or creativity. In each case, we can align our life choices both with those values *and* with the principle of responsibility. Will I be responsible by using my competence, by taking on challenges, or by finding creative solutions to areas such as work or family needs?

As we grew up, we learned a set of values, those qualities or standards that parents or caregivers considered important to our well-being and that of others. Families vary in the weight they place on certain values. Families often emphasize a variety of values, such as helping others, creativity, knowledge, financial security, or wealth accumulation. Early in our lives, we typically adopt our families' values, and as we mature, we often add our own. By selecting, interweaving, and prioritizing our values, we define who we are—or at least who we want to be. Just as we recognize people by their physical characteristics such as hair color, height, or the way they laugh, we also come to know people by the values they embody. As we get to know friends or people with whom we work, we begin to recognize what means the most to them. Do they crave excitement, care about the environment, or seek status? We evaluate others based on how well our values mesh with theirs. You might value personal time for creative work more than social activities while I might value relationships and family time more than professional recognition. We feel comfortable around people who share our most important values and often avoid those who don't. If you value financial security, for example, you may not enjoy associating with people whom you feel spend excessively.

Discovering Your Values

What is the set of values that anchors you? How would you want others to think of you? It's no coincidence that values are important to people who experience high levels of overall well-being. They know what their values are, and they consistently make decisions that are aligned with those values. To act in alignment with our values, we must first deeply understand what they are.

Try this: In the next 30 seconds, say out loud your five most important values. If you're like many people, you may find yourself stuttering or struggling to think. "*Uh* ... family ... financial security. *Umm* ... " Our values are typically not top of mind. That's why most values clarification exercises provide a "cheat sheet" list of common values.

Steve Pavlina,[3] a noted personal-development blogger, offers a list of 374 values on his website. Think2perform, the company founded by co-author Doug, created a pack of "values cards," akin to trading cards, each of which names and explains a value. They come with an exercise to help you identify your most important values.

> *You can order a set of Values cards on the think2perfrom website at* https://www.think2perform.com/tool-shop/tools/original-values-card-deck.
>
> *You can also access a free values exercise using think2perform's virtual values cards, which you'll find at* https://think2perform.com/our-approach/values.

Another way to begin exploring your values is to use the following exercise, "What Are Your Top Values?"

EXERCISE: WHAT ARE YOUR TOP VALUES?

Review this checklist of values. Begin by checking off the 15 that are most important to you. Then reflect and narrow that list to 10, and after more reflection, select your top five values. If you have an important value not on the list, use the blank spaces below to record other values. Don't rush through this exercise. Take some time to reflect on what really matters most to you.

☐ Adventure	☐ Autonomy	☐ Challenges	☐ Change
☐ Community	☐ Competence	☐ Competition	☐ Cooperation
☐ Creativity	☐ Decisiveness	☐ Diversity	☐ Ecology/Environment
☐ Education	☐ Ethics	☐ Excellence	☐ Excitement
☐ Fairness	☐ Fame	☐ Family	☐ Flexibility
☐ Freedom	☐ Friendship	☐ Happiness	☐ Health
☐ Helping Others	☐ Honesty	☐ Independence	☐ Integrity
☐ Leadership	☐ Loyalty	☐ Meaningful Work	☐ Money
☐ Order	☐ Philanthropy	☐ Play	☐ Pleasure
☐ Power	☐ Privacy	☐ Recognition	☐ Relationships
☐ Religion	☐ Safety	☐ Security	☐ Service
☐ Spirituality	☐ Status	☐ Wealth	☐ Work
☐_____	☐_____	☐_____	☐_____

---

[3]Steve Pavlina, "List of Values," November 29, 2004, https://www.stevepavlina.com/blog/2004/11/list-of-values/. Retrived August 8, 2017.

See Appendix A for a copy of the exercise, "What Are Your Top Values?"

When Eileen, the nurse anesthetist featured at the start of the chapter, reflected on her values, an exercise suggested by her life coach, she identified these five:

- Helping Others
- Family
- Friendship
- Community
- Health

Eileen and her coach discussed her values and explored areas where her life was and wasn't aligned with her most significant values. As a young woman, Eileen had chosen nursing because of her interest in helping people, so her current job seemed to be consistent with one of her top values. But when Eileen thought more deeply about her current job, she realized that her specialty area wasn't giving her the sense of helping people, since her patients were under anesthesia for most of their time with her. Though Eileen prided herself on keeping her patients safe and comfortable during their surgical procedures, she became aware that she missed working with patients who were in a conscious state, and felt that she needed more feedback from patients about whether she was succeeding in helping them. So Eileen began to consider studying to become a nurse practitioner, where she would be on the front lines of primary healthcare, and be better able to experience the results of her desire to help others.

Eileen also worked with her coach on ways to align her actions with the importance of family as a key value. Even though her son, daughter-in-law, and grandchildren had moved cross country, Eileen realized that she hadn't really "lost them." Given her relatively high income, Eileen could afford to get on a plane to the West Coast as often as she wanted. So her coach encouraged her to talk with her son and daughter-in-law to decide on a plan for regular visits that was comfortable for everyone. Eileen and her West Coast family mutually decided that it would be ideal if Eileen spent a week with them four times a year. They also decided how Eileen would spend holiday time with her son's family. Each year, Eileen would spend either Thanksgiving or

Christmas with her son's family, to accommodate her son's family need to spend certain major holiday time with his wife's family and her son's father. Eileen also figured out that she could afford to pay for airfare for her son and his family to visit her in Boston at least once a year.

Acting in alignment with Eileen's friendship value proved challenging for her. After all, Eileen had lost some friends in the wake of her divorce, and tried to foster new friendships through church groups and book clubs with little success. Eileen's coach suggested she use Facebook to locate old friends from high school and nursing school, and try to reestablish connections with them through social media. Before long, Eileen found someone on Facebook from her high school class who happened to be in charge of their high school class reunion, coming up in a few months' time, and the former classmate promptly sent her an invitation.

Eileen was tempted to skip the reunion, worried how she would look to others, given her weight gain, and uncomfortable about attending without a husband or boyfriend. Eileen's coach encouraged her to go anyway, pointing out that many of her classmates wouldn't be in ideal shape themselves. So Eileen decided to take the upcoming high school class reunion as a challenge to get in better shape. She revamped her eating plan to make it as healthy as possible, and started working out several times a week at a fitness center near her home. Feeling better about her progress in becoming more fit, Eileen bought a fabulous outfit for the reunion and even hired a makeup artist to help her make a glamorous entrance to the reunion. Though Eileen attended her high school class reunion without a date, she had the time of her life, and enjoyed reuniting with many high school friends, a few of whom turned out to live near Eileen. Within the next month or so, Eileen arranged lunches with several local long-lost high school friends. As she reconnected with her high school friends, she discovered mutual interests that opened up her world to new possibilities and activities in which she could become involved. Eileen also used Facebook to find a few nursing school friends. One particular friend, now a public health nurse, asked Eileen if she would volunteer to staff a local health fair which offered free health screenings, such as blood pressure checks and cholesterol screenings. Many health fair participants lacked resources for regular health exams, and Eileen felt she was helping others to recognize and address potentially dangerous health conditions. As Eileen became increasingly involved as a weekend health fair volunteer, she found herself part of an altruistic community of people who shared her values, and her connection with other volunteers helped her feel the sense of community that church groups and book clubs had failed to offer.

After a few months of weekly volunteer work, coupled with taking night classes to prepare her to become a nurse practitioner, Eileen went for a follow-up with her primary care physician. Surprisingly, Eileen had lost ten pounds, her blood pressure had dropped so much that her doctor cut back on her blood pressure medication, and her blood sugar level was averaging just above normal. These results motivated Eileen to work even more seriously on improving her health. Eileen started walking every day. She bought a pedometer to track her daily steps and set a goal of 10,000 steps a day. Eileen enjoyed the feedback she got from the pedometer, so much so that on days when she hadn't reached her goal, she walked around her condo at night after getting back from classes until she hit her target. Eileen's life was changing in many positive ways as she increasingly aligned her actions with her values.

Jim Loehr, a world-famous psychologist in the area of optimizing human performance, suggests an exercise in which you prioritize 10 common values you most want your life to reflect and compare that list with how much time and energy you invest in living in alignment with those values.[4] We adapted Loehr's valuable exercise to help you assess your current level of alignment with your values.

EXERCISE: VALUES AND BEHAVIOR ALIGNMENT

Step 1: In Column A, rank order from 1 to 10 the values you most want your life to represent.

Step 2: In Column B, rank order these values from 1 to 10 based on time and energy invested in each over the last year or so.

Step 3: Determine the difference between priority score for each top value and priority score for values in action.

---

[4]Jim Loehr, *The Only Way to Win: How Building Character Helps You Achieve More and Find Greater Fulfillment in Business and Life.* New York: Hyperion, 2012, p. 14–15.

Step 4: Subtract number in Column B "Investment" from number
    in Column A "Importance" and place in Column C "Alignment
    Level."

Step 5: Reflect on alignment or gap between priority of values and
    time/energy invested in each value. Is there alignment between
    what I believe is important in my life and my actual behavior?

Values	A: Importance What I Want My Life to Reflect (Rate importance from 1–10)	B: Investment Time and Energy I Spend (Rate from 1–10)	C: Alignment Alignment Level (Subtract Column B from Column A)
Wealth (how much money you have)			
Material Possessions (things you acquire)			
Family (as you understand your family, including non-traditional families)			
Social Status (degrees, job titles, awards, etc.)			
Health (physical and emotional)			
Power (feeling you control people and circumstances)			
Ethics (being honest, kind, generous, etc.)			
Fame (well-known by many people)			
Attractiveness (regarded as being beautiful or looking good)			
Work Performance (professional competence and mastery)			

In the Values and Behavior Alignment exercise, the larger the positive number in Column C, the more you invest in this value relative to its importance. The larger the negative number, the less you invest in that value relative to its importance. For instance, you may rank "Fame" as 10 in importance but 4 in your investment of time and energy. That leads to a gap of 6, which suggests that you may be spending too much time on a value that is not as important to you as other values. As another example, you may rate "Family" as 1 in importance, but a 5 in your investment. The gap of −4 indicates that you may not be investing enough time and energy in your family relative to their importance. A score at or close to zero (−2 to +2) suggests close alignment between a value's importance to you and the time and energy you invest in that value. Such numbers are only rough estimates of alignment between values and behavior. However, it's a useful way to begin to think about how meaningfully you are using your time and energy. And it will give you a head start in thinking about potential goals for yourself, before beginning the goal achievement process described in Chapter 3.

See Appendix B for a copy of the Values and Behavior Alignment exercise. You can also download a copy of the exercise (including a blank version that allows you to do the exercise using your own top 10 values) from the book Toolkit at www.leveragingfi.com.

＊＊＊＊＊＊

Eileen had come a long way from the unhappy woman who hated waking up in the morning. Focusing on her values helped Eileen discover her ideal self—the person she wanted to be at her best. In the process of taking those initial steps to live life more aligned with her values, Eileen was realizing the truth of what Helen Keller meant when she said, "Many persons have a wrong idea of what constitutes true happiness. It is not attained through self-gratification but through fidelity to a worthy purpose." Instead of engaging in recreational shopping in an effort to feel better, Eileen refocused her time on a meaningful pursuit—helping people understand and improve their health. Like Eileen, all of us can use our values as a springboard for discovering our purpose—the one true thing we believe is our reason for being.

CHAPTER THREE

Setting and Achieving Goals

The self is made, not given.

—Barbara Myerhoff

N ow in her mid-fifties, Donna Krone looks entirely too young to have had time to excel in three successive careers. Coincidentally, Donna's careers track with the three life areas emphasized in this book—financial health, physical health, and overall well-being (happiness). Donna graduated from college with a BS in nursing, and worked for five years as a nurse in a hospital. In that role, Donna saw the tragic results of uncontrollable medical conditions, and the life-threatening consequences of poor lifestyle choices made by patients over decades. Donna was a highly conscientious nurse. She advocated for her patients and made sure her patients and their families got all the information they needed to reduce their stress as they navigated the confusing hospital environment. Donna embraced the intellectual and coaching aspects of her nursing role, but always felt anxious about the technical aspects of her role. On the one hand, she thrived on acting as a liaison between busy doctors, who didn't always communicate very well, and patients and their families, who were desperate for clear and complete information about their situation. On the other hand, Donna didn't gain the satisfaction she thought she would in the fast-paced hospital environment where nurses had to get tasks done as quickly and efficiently as possible, often at the cost of patient relationships. Despite that, Donna continued working as a nurse until a serendipitous opportunity arose to pursue a career as a financial advisor with IDS, a financial services organization that eventually became American Express Financial Advisors, and later Ameriprise Financial.

Donna chose her new career as a financial advisor because she was attracted to the opportunity to help clients explore their dreams and clarify how financial choices could make them a reality. For Donna, it wasn't about the money. In learning the role of the financial advisor, Donna resonated with opportunities to coach people to achieve their life goals, both financial and nonfinancial, so she may have minimized the primary requirement of her job, which was to propose investments and optimize clients' financial gains. When Donna realized the primacy of selling financial products, she mastered the investment side of the business and spent the next 18 years as a successful financial services advisor helping people achieve their personal goals by making smart financial decisions. While working with clients, Donna was always aware that her major source of satisfaction was a result of the long-term relationships she formed with her clients. Donna continued to feel that spending most of her professional life dealing with money and investments was not deeply satisfying.

Over the course of a long career managing a successful financial advisory practice, Donna gradually came to believe that a more holistic approach to financial advice—one that would place more emphasis on values, purpose, and personal goals—was something she wanted to pursue. Donna began to take life coaching classes and work to integrate life coaching strategies into her financial advisory practice. Donna found it personally difficult to blend her approach to life coaching with financial advice.[1] Although Donna had learned a lot about money, to her family's benefit and that of her clients, she gradually realized

---

[1] Though Donna chose to specialize in life coaching, there are a growing number of financial advisors who coach their clients in discovering their purpose and values, and support them in setting holistic goals for financial, physical, and emotional well-being.

that in continuing as a financial advisor, she wasn't being fully true to her purpose. Donna's real passion was to help clients clarify their life purpose and implement goals that would address all-important areas of their lives. After 18 years as a successful financial advisor and considerable reflection on her life purpose and goals, Donna sold her practice and started from scratch as a life coach. Donna felt that her life purpose was to help others discover what mattered most to them. She sees her purpose as a life coach today as really about "setting her clients free internally." Donna considers herself successful when she sees that with her help, clients are freed to love their lives and love themselves.

LIVING ON PURPOSE

For Donna, each career shift was preceded by a period of deep reflection through which she became increasingly clear about her life purpose, and became better able to set more precise professional goals aligned with her deepest values. In doing that, Donna instinctively followed the Alignment Model, which as discussed in Chapter 2, maps out the key challenge of living a good life, that is, doing what we need to do to make our real selves (Frame 3) as close as possible to our ideal selves (Frame 1)—the way we want to be, based on principles and values.

The journey of "making the ideal real" necessarily requires an intermediate stop at Frame 2—Goals. The foundation of our ideal selves, principles, and values is broad and general. Frame 2 is all about defining concrete behaviors (Frame 3) that reflect our principles and values (Frame 1). As you'll recall, Frame 2 includes different levels of goals:

- Purpose—a high-level goal that represents what we want our life to mean
- Goals—specific desired achievements aligned with our most important values

Scientists who study behavior tell us that humans have an innate need to make sense out of their lives. We constantly develop theories to explain why events happen as they do. We have an even deeper need to understand the meaning of our lives. How do our day-to-day events combine to create a coherent whole? What is the point of doing what we do? If we can begin to answer those questions, we have the beginning of our highest goal—our life's purpose. Everyone's life purpose is distinctively their own, but any purpose worth having is consistent with universal principles. Though service to others is frequently part of one's purpose, you don't have to be another Mother Teresa to serve a worthwhile purpose. Purpose is about finding how to use your gifts and skills in some personally meaningful way. Your purpose may be to create art, to be a great parent, invent new products, or become a philosopher. Your purpose is what makes your life worth living. And you get to decide what that is.

National Geographic fellow and author Dan Buettner has extensively studied "Blue Zones," areas of exceptional longevity in different parts of the world. One of these Blue Zones, Okinawa, is an island in southernmost Japan. According to Buettner, Okinawans in their nineties and beyond attribute their long lives in part to their "ikigai"—their purpose, their reason for being. Okinawans literally define ikigai as their "reason for getting up in the morning."[2] Other researchers support Buettner's findings. Residents of the Japanese village with the world's highest percentage of centenarians explained to authors Héctor Garcia and Francesc Miralles that finding ikigai is key to a happy life. Garcia and Miralles also believe that ikigai is the reason why many Japanese don't retire, since according to their studies of the Okinawan culture, the essence of ikigai is to remain active doing enjoyable work.[3] Of course, Okinawans do not represent the only culture that emphasizes the benefits of living in alignment with your purpose. For instance, in the Costa Rican "Blue Zone" of Nicoya, elders emphasize the importance of a concept very similar to ikigai, the "plan de vida."[4]

In addition to field studies such as these, controlled scientific research has validated the relationship between sense of purpose

---

[2] Dan Buettner, *The Blue Zones: 9 Lessons for Living Longer from the People Who've Lived the Longest*, 2nd Edition. National Geographic Partners LLC, 2011.

[3] Héctor García and Francesc Miralles, *Ikigai: The Japanese Secret to a Long and Happy Life*. Penguin Books, 2017.

[4] Dan Buettner, *The Blue Zones: 9 Lessons for Living Longer from the People Who've Lived the Longest*, 2nd Edition. National Geographic Partners LLC, 2011.

and longevity. For example, a study conducted at the University of Rochester Medical Center found that having a purpose in life reduced the risk of dying for people of all ages. Their findings imply that developing and maintaining a strong purpose in life is as important when people are young as it is at much older ages.[5]

The research on the relationship between sense of purpose, health, and overall well-being is undeniable. But perhaps the most compelling argument for the importance of purpose in our lives is captured in a story by Richard Leider, nationally recognized executive-life coach and best-selling author of *The Power of Purpose*, who tells of a question he was once asked by the elder of an African tribe: "What are the two most important days of your life?" Richard answered, "The day I was born, and the day I will die." The elder told him, "You are wrong. The two most important days in your life are the day you were born, and the day you determine why you were born."[6]

What exactly is purpose? According to Richard Leider:

> *Our purpose is the essence of who we are and what makes us unique. Our purpose is an active expression of the deepest dimension within us—where we have a profound sense of who we are and why we're here. Purpose is the aim around which we structure our lives, a source of direction and energy. Through the lens of purpose, we are able to see ourselves—and our future—more clearly .... Purpose is what gives life a meaning.*[7]

Many of us may, in Richard Leider's words, " . . . believe we have a purpose but are challenged by what it may be or how to find out."[8] If you're not already clear about your life's purpose, and have a longing to find out, be prepared to spend some time in reflection. To help you better understand your life purpose, use the exercise "What Is Your Life's Purpose?," based on Richard Leider's work, to help provide you more insight about your life's purpose.

[5] Patrick L. Hill and Nicholas A. Turiano, "Purpose in Life as a Predictor of Mortality across Adulthood," *Psychological Science*, 2014 Jul; 25(7): 1482–1486.
[6] Richard J. Leider, as told during keynote presentation at think2perform Annual Conference, Minneapolis, MN, October 2016.
[7] Richard J. Leider, *The Power of Purpose: Find Meaning, Live Longer, Better*, 2nd edition (San Francisco: Berrett-Koehler Publishers, 2010).
[8] Ibid.

EXERCISE: WHAT IS YOUR LIFE'S PURPOSE?[9]

Take some time to reflect on the questions below. Answering these questions can help you clarify the high-level meaning and direction that you would like your life to take. You may also find it useful to discuss your responses with a close family member or friend.

1. **What are my talents?**

2. **What am I passionate about?**

3. **What do I obsess about, daydream about?**

4. **What do I wish I had more time to put energy into?**

5. **What needs doing in the world that I'd like to put my talents to work on?**

6. **What are the main areas in which I'd like to invest my talents?**

7. **What environments or settings feel most natural to me?**

8. **In what work and life situations am I most comfortable expressing my talents?**

Your purpose may already be clear. Even if you don't already know your purpose, awareness about your purpose may come to you quickly. It may also evolve gradually, as it did for Donna Krone. Richard Leider

[9]Adapted from Richard J. Leider, *Repacking Your Bags: Lighten Your Load for the Rest of Your Life* (San Francisco: Berrett-Koehler Publishers, 1995).

suggests occasionally taking a day away from your normal routine to reflect on what really matters to you. Take along a copy of the Life Purpose exercise, a pen and some colored pencils, and sheets of blank paper.

You can find a copy of the exercise "What Is Your Life's Purpose?" in Appendix C or you can download a copy from the book Toolkit at www.leveragingfi.com.

Maybe your thoughts will come to you in words. You might also find yourself doodling or making sketches that capture your response to the worksheet questions. After you've responded to the worksheet questions, put them aside for a few days. Then return to those questions. Ask yourself if they still strike a chord in you. Would you answer them the same way today as you did the first time? What would you add or change about your responses to the Life Purpose exercise? Taking time to engage in this process of discovery may be one of the most important things you do as part of reading this book. You may also discover that taking the time to explore your life purpose is not just a serious process—it's also a lot of fun. Focusing on your life purpose can help you feel lighter and happier as you release obstacles to happiness and move closer to making your ideal self your real self.

Once you're feeling confident about your life purpose, you're much more likely to fulfill your purpose if you can clearly imagine what your life would be like when you are acting in alignment with your purpose. In Doug Lennick and Roy Geer's book, *How to Get What You Want and Remain True to Yourself*, they discuss a self-image theory, which says, "You will become what you believe yourself to be."[10] Doug and Roy advocate taking advantage of a powerful practice used by elite athletes—using their minds to visualize themselves performing perfectly. This practice has become commonplace in sports training, and it's just as effective when it comes to living a happy and fulfilled life. In fact, visualizing life purpose may be even more important than visualizing perfect performance in sports, where athletes typically only need to operate at peak performance for a short period of time. Life is a full-time sport, so the impact of visualizing ourselves successfully living our purpose 24/7 can be profound. To help visualize what it would be like to live in alignment with your life purpose, use the following exercise.

[10] Doug Lennick and Roy Geer, *How to Get What You Want and Remain True to Yourself*, Lerner Publications Company, 1995.

EXERCISE: VISUALIZE YOURSELF LIVING YOUR PURPOSE[11]

- Sit or lie down in a relaxing spot.
- Take some deep breaths, and focus in turn on each part of your body from head to toe, allowing your muscles to loosen and relax as you concentrate on each part of your body.
- While continuing to breathe naturally, imagine yourself near the end of your life.
- Reflect on your life to this point in time. Throughout the years, what has given your life the most meaning and purpose?
- Allow yourself to feel a sense of contentment as you realize that you are fulfilling your purpose.
- After spending a few minutes in reflection, open your eyes and return to the present, while maintaining a sense of satisfaction about a life well-lived.

You can find a copy of the exercise "Visualize Yourself Living Your Purpose" in Appendix D.

You can also access an audio guide for visualizing your life purpose from the book Toolkit at www.leveragingfi.com.

Hopefully, by now you have clarified your life purpose, and can express it to yourself and others you trust. Your life purpose may evolve over time, but for now, it's enough that you feel good about your sense of purpose as you understand it at this point in your life. With your purpose in mind, your next step on the way to financial, physical, and emotional well-being is to set goals.

WHAT ON EARTH IS "WIDDY WIFFY"?

Our approach to goal achievement is called the WDYWFY model. WDYWFY is an acronym for "What Do You Want For Yourself?" WDYWFY is pronounced "widdy wiffy." Co-author Roy Geer originated the model in the 1960s. Over the last 50 years or so, thousands of people have used the WDYWFY model to help them decide what they want for themselves—and successfully achieve their goals. As Roy shared with co-author Doug Lennick in late 1974, when Doug was

---

[11] Based on an exercise discussed by Jim Loehr in his book, *The Only Way to Win: How Building Character Drives Higher Achievement and Greater Fulfillment in Business and Life* (New York: Hyperion, 2012).

F I G U R E **3.1**   **WIDYWFY**

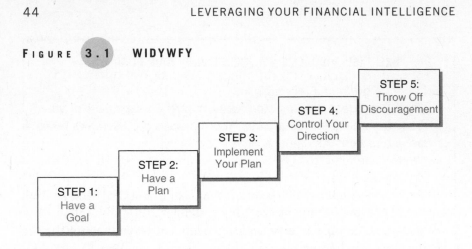

22 and Roy was 47, goal achievement is as simple as implementing five profoundly simple steps. Doug soon realized goal achievement is indeed simple but is definitely not easy. WDYWFY consists of those five profoundly simple steps (Figure 3.1).

A friendly warning: The WDYWFY model is truly simple. But as already said, it doesn't mean it's easy. Setting and achieving goals in any area of life is not easy. For example, think about Americans' most common New Year's resolutions, such as losing weight, quitting smoking, or saving more money. Only 8 percent of those who make New Year's resolutions feel they have succeeded in achieving their resolution.[12]

WDYWFY is a process with a proven track record of helping people actually achieve their goals. WDYWFY is a model you can use to dramatically boost your odds of achieving your financial, health, and happiness goals.

STEP 1: HAVE A GOAL

People who know what they want have a much better chance of getting it than when they don't know what they want. So an obvious first step is to have a goal. Let's clarify what a goal is—and isn't: A goal is something we want for ourselves. But not everything we want is a goal. There are many things we want in life, but to have them, we need to understand

---

[12]Dan Diamond. "Just 8% of People Achieve Their New Year's Resolutions. Here's How They Do It," Forbes.com, January 1, 2013, https://www.forbes.com/sites/dandiamond/2013/01/01/just-8-of-people-achieve-their-new-years-resolutions-heres-how-they-did-it/#515c0bae596b.

what we must do to achieve them. To turn *wants* into *goals*, *wants* must pass the "acid test."

The acid test for a goal is the ability to answer two questions:

1. Am I able to pay the price to reach my goal?
2. Am I willing to invest the time, money, or other resources needed to reach my goal?

Able and willing are two different things. Doug uses this example to make the distinction between the two: Doug, a basketball fan and amateur player, would love to be able to slam-dunk a basketball into a regulation hoop. He is very willing to do whatever it would take: coaching, practice, anything. But no matter how willing Doug is to invest in trying to reach that goal, he isn't able. Doug's doesn't have the physiology to perform like an elite player, and no amount of coaching or practice will make that possible. Doug's dream of slam-dunking the basketball will always be just that—a want that doesn't pass the acid test, and therefore is not a goal.

One of the major benefits of the acid test is to help you prioritize the importance of a number of potentially worthwhile goals. For example, if your top value is "family happiness," you may need to postpone training for your adventure-fueled desire to climb Mt. Everest, which would take you away from your family for extended periods of time. You also need to be realistic about your capacity to work on multiple goals at the same time. Everything you want may be meaningful and aligned with your values, but your available time and resources may limit how much you can accomplish in any given time frame. Here's an example of why the acid test is important: Those people who achieve their financial goals tend to invest their money. Those people who don't achieve their financial goals tend to spend their money. It's the same with other goals, say for health and happiness. Those people who achieve their life goals tend to invest their time in working to accomplish them. Those people who don't achieve their life goals tend to spend their time in an undisciplined way.

Use the worksheet "Turning Wants into Goals" to reflect on potential goals (What I Want), determine what you would need to do to accomplish each goal (Key Activities), and decide whether you can and will do what it takes to make what you want a reality (the Acid Test).

WORKSHEET: TURNING WANTS INTO GOALS

What I Want ...	Key Activities *"Must Do" actions needed to accomplish this goal.*	Does What You Want Pass the Acid Test? *Can I and will I do all it takes to turn this want into a goal?*
Financially	• • • •	
For My Health	• • • •	
For My Overall Happiness	• • • •	
Other Want:	• • •	

You can find a copy of the "Turning Wants into Goals" worksheet in Appendix E. You can also download copies from the book Toolkit at www.leveragingfi.com.

Fortunately, many things you want will qualify as goals if you are both willing and able to do what it takes to get where you want to go. Co-author Ryan Goulart tells this story about trying to turn a long-held want into a goal.

RYAN'S STORY

In December 2015, my wife, Joanie, and I began planning for a big trip to Europe in 2016. It had been about 10 years since either of us had traveled overseas, and we'd never been to Europe together. I am an avid soccer fan and had never been to France, where the 2016

European Championship was to be played. It had always been a dream of mine to be able to see this tournament. The tournament was to be held in June 2016. This would give Joanie and me enough time to save the necessary funds to travel to France and have enough money to see other sights while there. What made the trip even more inviting was that one of my best friends from high school was doing fieldwork for his doctoral dissertation in nearby Germany. So, we reworked our budget and cut back on optional spending to save for our trip.

Hints that we needed to adjust our plans came to light only a few months before we were scheduled to fly to France. We thought we were on track with our vacation savings, but traveling in France during the high season and dealing with inflated prices caused by the soccer tournament was turning out to be more expensive than we could afford. And my friend wasn't going to be able to meet us in France in June because of a conflict with his field research schedule.

So Joanie and I began to research other options and thought it would be fun to celebrate our September wedding anniversary in Europe, ideally in some areas that were more affordable than France. The delay would give us more time to save money, and would be cheaper overall, because of the time of year and our decision to visit less expensive places.

We decided that we would visit Amsterdam, Cologne, Hamburg, and Berlin, where my friend was still working. Unfortunately, European soccer was on an off-season break during our trip, so seeing an international soccer tournament is still a dream. I was disappointed, but our goal adjustment process was worth it, because Joanie and I were able to take a great trip together and we got to spend time with my friend.

Though Ryan and Joanie ran into some turbulence on their way to Europe, their travel goal clearly passed the acid test: They were willing and able to do what it took to make their trip a reality.

Goals Need to Be Connected to Values and Purpose

Achieving goals works best when goals are clearly connected to one's principles, values, and purpose. For example, in Donna Krone's case, as she found herself wanting to integrate coaching into her financial planning practice, she set a goal of enrolling in a coaching certification program. To have a happy life, it's helpful to ensure that the majority of your goals align with your principles, values, and purpose. This doesn't mean you can't set goals that may seem to be "selfish." In fact, goal achievement is a rightfully selfish process, provided the goals are aligned with universal principles (integrity, responsibility, compassion, forgiveness) and personal values (for example, family, happiness, wisdom, service, and health.) Co-author Roy Geer had always believed that "having fun" is a legitimate value, and that as humans we're meant to have fun in the process of living in alignment.

Best Practices for Developing and Achieving Goals

You may have heard of a goal achievement study supposedly conducted at either Harvard University or Yale University. According to reports about the study, college graduates who wrote down their career goals were found years later to have been much more likely to have reached their goals than graduates who didn't write down their goals. The catch is that this study doesn't exist. When Gail Matthews, a psychologist at Dominican University, discovered that the written goals study was an urban legend, she decided to conduct her own research on the subject.[13] Participants in Matthews' study were randomly assigned to groups which were asked to engage in different tasks related to goal achievement. Matthews' research validated the importance of written goals. But the study also found that additional factors influence successful goal achievement. Matthews' research revealed the following:

- Only 43 percent of participants who were asked just to think about goals they hoped to accomplish either achieved their goals or were halfway there.
- Participants who wrote down their goals achieved significantly more goals than those who did not.
- 62 percent of participants who wrote down their goals and action commitments and shared their goal commitments with a friend either accomplished their goals or were at least halfway there.

[13] Dominican University, "Study Focuses on Strategies for Achieving Goals, Resolutions," press release, Dominican.edu, 2015, http://www.dominican.edu/dominicannews/study-highlights-strategies-for-achieving-goals.

- The participants who were most successful were those who wrote down their goals and action commitments and sent weekly progress reports to a friend, with 76 percent either accomplishing their goals or being at least halfway there.

This study shows not just the power of written goals, but also demonstrates the even greater cumulative effect of writing down goals, committing publicly to specific actions, and being accountable to someone supportive as you work toward achieving your goals.

The authors' work with thousands of clients confirms the Matthews' study results. Documenting goals in writing and enlisting support from others, for instance a coach, partner, or spouse, greatly increases the likelihood that you will reach your goals.

STEP 2: HAVE A PLAN

So far we've been talking mostly about the process of setting a goal. The second step in the WDYWFY model is to have a plan for reaching your goal. Analyze your goal and determine everything you need to do to accomplish your goal. Ideally you will already have identified key activities in order to apply the acid test. As part of developing a goal achievement plan, take another look at your key activities list to be sure you have included all "must dos" for reaching your goal. Key activities answer as many of the following questions as possible:

- What is the action?
- When will I do it?
- How long will I do it?
- How frequently will I do it (if more than once)?
- With whom will I do it (if someone other than just myself)?

Here is an example of key activities that were part of Ryan and Joanie Goulart's plan for their September 2016 European trip:

- Joanie must make plane reservations by April 15.
- Ryan must put together an itinerary and schedule for the trip by May 30.
- Joanie must book lodgings for all destinations by June 30.
- Together we must save enough money each month through August 30 to fund our total travel budget.

Use the Goal Achievement Plan worksheet for recording key activities needed to accomplish your goal. You can find a blank copy in Appendix E. You can also download copies from the book Toolkit at www.leveragingfi.com.

EXAMPLE: GOAL ACHIEVEMENT PLAN

My Goal: Attain a healthy weight, meaning I must lose 20 pounds within 6 months.		
Key Activities "I Must Do":	Eat healthy meals; do not skip breakfast. Limit alcohol to one glass of wine with dinner, weekends only. Fast-walk 30 minutes five days a week, Mon–Fri; "10,000 steps" 7X/week. Sleep at least 7.5 hours a night. Go to bed by 10 PM.	
Resources I Need to Perform My Key Activities:	Produce, eggs, and grass-fed meats from local farms Money for increase in cost of higher quality foods Fitbit fitness tracker to motivate and maintain accountability Money for health coach	
People I Need to Support Me and How	Name	Support I'll request
	Julio, my health coach	Help with eating plan; ideas about exercise; encouragement
	John, my husband	Understand why I need to go to bed earlier; don't bring junk food into the house; help with extra money for healthier food
How I'll Track Progress	Review progress against plan every Friday at 3:00 PM; Meet biweekly with my health coach to get feedback and discuss results.	
How I'll Manage Emotions	When I feel discouraged, I will take 10 minutes to do a deep-breathing meditation and visualize myself as a healthy, fit person.	

Also think about specific resources you need—people, equipment, and so on, needed to achieve your key activities. Consider any other resources you need to achieve your key activities. As part of your plan, ask a coach, mentor, or other support person for their help. If they agree, solicit their feedback on the value of your goal and their suggestions about any changes or additions to your key activities. Entering key activities and any related tasks in your calendar will increase the odds you'll stay on track with your plan. Also schedule regular check-ins with a coach, mentor, or other support person to promote accountability and commitment and to help you adapt your plan as needed.

STEP 3: IMPLEMENT YOUR PLAN

One of the best ways to ensure you'll implement your plan is to schedule key activities and related tasks. It's not enough to say you're going to visit your mother at the nursing home several times a week. You need to put key activities in your calendar, just like you would any other "official" activity. When it comes to implementing key activities, don't leave anything to chance. If you know what actions you could take that would help you achieve a goal, put it on the calendar. A few years ago, Joe, one of the author Doug Lennick's clients, told Doug he wanted to get in shape. Here's how the conversation went:

Doug: What are you going to do to get in shape?

Joe: I'm going to go to the health club.

Doug: What are you going to do there?

Joe: Work out on some machines and run a few miles on the treadmill.

Doug: How often are you going?

Joe: I think three times a week.

Doug: How long are you going to spend there?

Joe: Uh, well, maybe 90 minutes.

Doug: When are you going to go there?

Joe: Whenever I can.

Doug: You say you are going to go three times a week for 90 minutes, and you know what you're going to do when you get there, but you won't really go. How often does it happen that you have nothing to do, and you think, "I'll go to the gym." Let me tell you a plan that will work. Take me as an example: I lift weights twice a week. I play basketball twice a week. I play tennis once a week. They are all on the calendar. Do I miss doing them sometimes? Yes. But would I go if they weren't on the calendar? No. So, Joe, you need to put your schedule for going to the gym on your calendar and treat it as seriously as any other commitment.

While you implement your plan, take a few minutes every day to visualize yourself successfully achieving your goal. Also anticipate any potential obstacles you may encounter along the way and think about how you could prevent or overcome them.

By consistently working on key activities, the things that seem hard to do, or require sacrifice to accomplish a goal, can become sources of satisfaction. Research on happiness has shown that one of the characteristics of the happiest people is that they set goals and gain satisfaction from the process of working toward them. When we implement the goal achievement process, the anticipation of achievement allows us to enjoy not just the destination but the process. Especially when goals are aligned with values, we feel a sense of pride in doing something worthwhile and gain satisfaction when it's done well.

STEP 4: CONTROL DIRECTION

Controlling direction is about tracking progress and redirecting as needed. Implementing an imperfect plan perfectly won't work. Only rarely do we implement a goal achievement plan that doesn't require change. "Control direction" is a critical WDYWFY step because it allows us to keep score and make adjustments as needed. Consider this example: If an airplane takes off from New York for Los Angeles, it is off course 97 percent of the time. Air traffic controllers track where the plane is and provide input that calls for frequent directional changes, as well as altitude changes, often to provide minimum safe separation from other aircraft or to accommodate weather systems. The plane takes off and lands in the right places, but without keeping score and redirecting as needed, it might end up in Alaska instead of LA. Like a successful flight plan, Ryan and Joanie Goulart's plan for their European trip succeeded largely because they were able to recognize when their plan was going off track and change course as needed.

STEP 5: THROW OFF DISCOURAGEMENT

Working on a goal, like everything we do in life, triggers emotions. Take the example of a goal to lose weight. You've worked out every day. You're being careful about your diet. You're getting enough sleep. But when you step on the scale for a weekly weigh-in, you haven't lost an ounce.

It's easy to feel discouraged, and in the throes of that frustration, you might impulsively order a pizza, which obviously does nothing to further your goal. Discouragement is only one of many emotions we may feel in the course of implementing a goal. We might feel scared that things will never improve, or we may feel anxious about what it will be like to succeed. (For example, "Who will I be, if I'm not the funny chubby one at the party?") We may hit a milestone on the way to our goal that shows we've made a lot of progress, and become so excited that we get off track. Say that weekly weigh-in shows you've lost five pounds this week. Time for a piece of cheesecake, right? Wrong. "Throw off discouragement" is shorthand for sticking to your plan no matter what you're feeling, positive or negative. You will always have to deal with emotions. You can't control them as they rise up in you. But you can control how you think and what you do in the presence of those difficult to deal with emotions. If you're anxious, what should you do? Do your key activities. If you're ecstatic, what should you do? Do your key activities. It's that simple. As we've said before, it's simple but not easy. It's not easy, but you can do it. You *can* reach your goals. As Dr. Louis Pasteur, the famous nineteenth-century microbiologist, said, "Let me tell you the secret that has led me to my goal. My strength lies solely in my tenacity."

* * * * * *

The Alignment Model and the WDYWFY Goal Achievement Model are proven approaches to help you maintain and enhance your financial, physical, and emotional well-being. In the next section of the book you will learn how to apply these powerful models to set and achieve mutually reinforcing goals at the intersection of money, health, and happiness. As you work on financial goals, you'll achieve greater financial security. You'll also discover opportunities to achieve health goals. As you focus on health, you'll notice you have the stamina and motivation to be more productive and successful in your work. As you work on happiness goals, you'll find that all areas of your life, including financial, physical, and emotional health, are improving every day.

CHAPTER FOUR

Money

Wealth is the ability to fully experience life.
—Henry David Thoreau

Michelle Arpin Begina knows a lot about financial stress. She grew up in the 1970s and 1980s in a family with chronic money problems. Her mom came from humble beginnings and was thrifty by nature, though her husband never allowed her to participate in significant family financial decisions. Michelle's dad had come from a wealthy family, but unfortunately, he was a lifelong spendthrift. Whenever her dad had money, he spent it—sometimes on whopping extravagances such as planes and boats. When Michelle was 10 years old, her parents were so behind on mortgage payments that they almost lost their home. In 1985, her dad paid $185,000 in cash for a yacht. When Michelle asked her dad about money for college, he said he couldn't afford it. Michelle's dad didn't express remorse or seem to think he had a responsibility to help her. His attitude seemed to be that it wasn't important for a girl to attend college. That's when Michelle realized she was on her own. Determined to keep her dream of going to college alive, she got a job right out of high school, moved away from home and went to college at night. Michelle's experience of financial stress was far from over. Struggling to pay for college and make ends meet on a low salary, her anxiety was, in her words, "off the chart."

Michelle has come a long way since those stressful early years. Now a successful financial services executive and certified retirement coach, Michelle says, "I do what I do now so people don't make the huge money mistakes that I witnessed as a child." She and her husband, Mike, have put those painful lessons from Michelle's childhood into practice in managing their family finances. For example, they are very disciplined about saving for their two sons' college expenses. "One thing that makes me happiest," Michelle says, "is knowing that, independent of scholarships or loans, full resources for college are available for our children. We've been contributing enough to their 529 accounts to send them to any college that accepts them."

FROM MISERY TO WISDOM

Chapter 1 highlighted extensive research that confirms how widespread financial stress is: At least 75 percent of us feel some degree of financial stress. We tend to feel financial stress whether our income or net worth is objectively low or high. If we don't have enough money, or like Michelle Begina's dad, we'd have enough money if we didn't overspend, we feel stress. Even if we have enough money, we still worry, because we know that any number of unforeseen events could affect our financial security. We also know from research that financial stress has an outsized negative impact on other key areas of life. As financial stress increases, our ability to effectively manage emotions such as fear, anxiety, denial, or resentment falls. According to neuroscientists, when we are feeling stress, the part of the brain that processes emotions, the *amygdala*, is probably on overdrive, disabling the logical part of our brain, *the pre-frontal cortex*, which under high-stress conditions is barely operating, if at all. Overwhelmed by negative or competing emotions, our decision-making and behavior becomes increasingly irrational. And when we're in the throes of an irrational decision-making process, we do things that harm not just our finances, but our physical health and overall happiness. Figure 4.1 shows the process by which financial stress leads to poor life outcomes. Notice that the graphic is in the shape of an "M," which appropriately stands for "misery," since the basic result of financial stress is that it makes us miserable.

FIGURE **4.1**   MISERY: IMPACT OF FINANCIAL STRESS

Unfortunately, financial stress not only makes us feel miserable emotionally, it also can make us feel miserable physically. When authors Doug Lennick and Ryan Goulart asked psychiatrist Helen Riess, of Harvard Medical School, if financial stress affected physical health, she emphatically responded, "The answer to that question is yes." Riess went on to say, "Stress is not just a mental state. It's also a physical state. All kinds of physical issues, including heart disease, diabetes, and obesity can result." Riess also pointed out, "Our brains are wired to perceive danger. And the dangers we perceive today are usually related to health, relationship, or financial issues." Chapter 1 noted numerous scientific studies that support Riess's conclusions. Other professionals confirm that misery can be part of the intersection of money, health, and happiness. Chiropractor Moses Smith, owner of the highly successful wellness clinic, Moe Body Works, in Minneapolis, knows as well as anyone how important it is to maintain positive health practices. But even Dr. Moe, with all her health expertise, periodically ends up on the misery track. "When I get stressed financially," Dr. Moe says, "I stop exercising, and emotionally I start to struggle."

Diana Iannarone is an author, former Fortune 100 executive, and founder in 2005 of Redthorn Solutions, a life reinvention coaching practice which specializes in helping people break the bonds of unhealthy or exploitative relationships and situations. Diana is widely lauded for helping countless people reach their full personal and professional potential by examining the beliefs that block their passage to a fulfilled life.

As a financial executive and a single mother throughout her early career, Diana has been financially disciplined all through her adult life. Despite her considerable skills, Diana still experiences times when financial stress affects her health and happiness. In a 2016 conversation with author Doug Lennick, Diana shared, "When I am more worried about money, I notice I don't keep myself as socially active. I exercise less and tend to be somewhat demotivated."

Even though Diana objectively "has enough" financially, she is not immune from occasional financial worries and the negative impact financial stress can have on anyone's physical and emotional well-being. To minimize the emotional highs and lows of financial health, Diana conscientiously aligns her spending and cash flow.

No one wants to be miserable, financially, physically, or emotionally. So, if we want to feel better, we need to reverse the cycle of misery. We need to turn misery upside down and access our wisdom. To move from misery to wisdom, the key is to reduce financial stress.

As Figure 4.2 shows, when we lower financial stress, we can turn the "M" of misery upside down, triggering a chain of events that becomes the "W" of wisdom. When we're able to reduce financial stress, our emotional competence increases, decreasing the likelihood that we'll make irrational decisions or act against our best interests. When we

FIGURE 4.2 WISDOM: REDUCING FINANCIAL STRESS

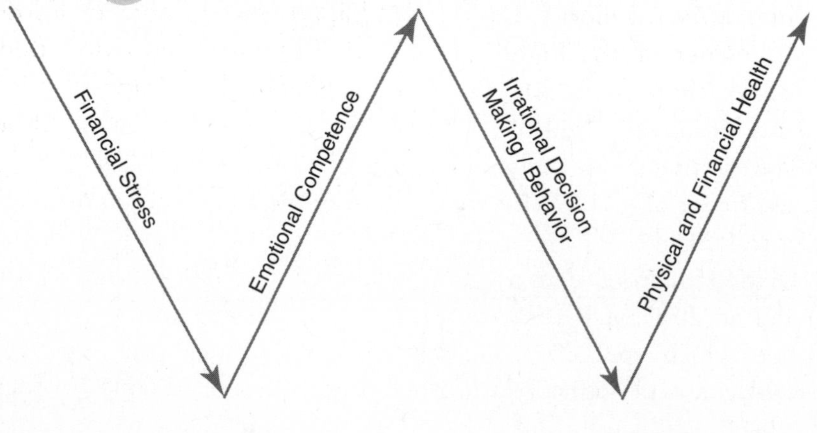

make rational decisions about finances, the better off we are, not just financially, but in all other areas of life affected by our financial decisions, such as health and happiness.

THE SECRET OF WISDOM: PREPARING FOR THE CERTAINTY OF UNCERTAINTY

In Doug's previous book, *Financial Intelligence*, he described the tragic circumstances of his mother's sudden death in 1996. Doug says that more than any other previous life experience, his mother's loss really brought home the "certainty of uncertainty." He was rudely reminded that two things are true. One: We all will die. Two: We don't know when and how. But because we are uncertain about the second, we try to ignore the first. And that's the situation that many of us put ourselves in financially. Because we don't know when or how things will happen, we try to kid ourselves that they won't happen. But trying to deny that difficult situations are likely to happen during our lives doesn't work. At a physiological level, we always experience some emotional discomfort because of life's inevitable uncertainty, and that in turn can contribute to chronic stress. To minimize stress and the damage stress causes, we all need to prepare for life's predictably unpredictable events.

Preparing for the certainty of uncertainty is the essence of the Smart Money Philosophy, an approach to financial planning that is one of the best ways to reduce financial stress. In addition to preparing us financially for life's twists and turns, the Smart Money Philosophy has two added benefits: By planning for the certainty of uncertainty, we are better able to ensure that our values will be put into action. When we plan, we have better access to our rational brain, and we're less likely to make ill-considered, emotionally driven decisions. And by putting our plans in writing, as discussed in Chapter 3, we have a concrete reminder of the financial strategies that we've decided will support our values and goals. Reviewing our plans regularly, especially with a trusted advisor, can reinforce our ability to maintain alignment with those values and goals, making it less likely we'll make impulsive financial decisions in moments of fear or excitement.

WHAT CAN'T YOU KNOW?

When it comes to life events and their financial implications, there are a lot of uncertainties. There is so much that we can't predict, no matter how smart we are. To be prepared for such unpredictable events, we must first understand *what we can't know*.

You can't know what's going to happen with the overall economy. This includes economic factors such as inflation, employment, interest rates, the price of oil, GDP, and so on. Let's discuss a few examples from the time of the Great Recession. You couldn't know that the price of oil would go to $145 a barrel in July 2008. Nor could you know that two months later, it would be trading under $100 a barrel. Or that, even with a large drop in oil price, the price of gas would still be 60 percent higher than the previous year. You couldn't know that unemployment would be at a 25-year high in August 2008, eventually exceeding 10 percent by the end of 2009. You couldn't know that consumer inflation would hit a 17-year high in August 2008. And you couldn't know how any of that would affect your job security, your salary, or your family's expenses for basic needs.

You can't know what's going to happen in the real estate market. For most Americans, the lion's share of their net worth is in their home equity. Given that 63% of United States residents own their homes (or are mortgage holders), most of us are deeply involved in the real estate market. It's a fact that values of homes go up and down. There's no way to know exactly how much or when, but the last 20 years should have taught us that the strength of real estate markets can vary widely depending on time or region. For several years prior to 2006 there were four real estate markets that people believed could not go down: Florida, California, Arizona, and Las Vegas, Nevada. Those four regions were hardest hit by the steep housing decline of 2007 through 2009. However, as of 2016, home prices in areas such as Miami, Las Vegas, and parts of Arizona and California are now seeing the sharpest gains.[1] Despite significant rises in home prices in coastal

[1]Troy McMullen, "Areas hit hardest by the real estate bust are now seeing the highest gains," https://www.washingtonpost.com/realestate/2016/08/17/66bf7d86-536d-11e6-88eb-7dda4e2f2aec_story.html, August, 2016. Retrieved April 18, 2017.

urban areas, across the United States overall "home prices in 3 out of 5 metropolitan areas *remain below* their pre-recession peak," according to a 2017 report by the Joint Center for Housing Studies of Harvard University.[2]

You can't know what's going to happen in the financial markets. You couldn't know that in the fall of 2008, the financial markets would collectively lose more than 30% of their value, threatening retirement savings, even those in seemingly safe investments such as money market funds.[3] You couldn't know that the Dow Jones Industrial Average (DJIA) of representative company stocks would reach 14,164 on October 9, 2007, and then fall by March 9, 2009, to 6,547, down almost 54 percent in less than 18 months. After such a catastrophic decline, it would have been hard to imagine that by January 25, 2017, the DJIA would reach 20,000, up almost 205% in a period of about eight years.

What will happen to future financial markets? Will they go up? Down? You just can't know with certainty. But we predict the answer is yes. They will go up, and they will go down.

You can't know what's going to happen around the globe. As of 2017 when this book was being written, global political uncertainty seemed more widespread than at any time since World War II. You can't know what military conflicts might erupt across the globe. For example, you might be unnerved by North Korea's progress in developing the capability to deliver a nuclear weapon atop a long-range ballistic missile that can reach many parts of the United States. You can't know how global adversaries might capitalize on emerging technologies to wage new forms of warfare, such as Russia's cyberattack intended to influence the 2016 U.S. presidential election. You can't know the impact on the U.S. economy of Great Britain's potential exit from the European Union or how changes in the United States administration's policies will affect global alliances and economics. For instance, you can't know how potential changes in U.S. immigration

---

[2] "The State of the Nation's Housing 2017," *Joint Center for Housing Studies of Harvard University,* 2017, http://www.jchs.harvard.edu/research/state_nations_housing, 2017. Retrieved June 16, 2017.
[3] Paul Kosakowski, "The Fall of the Market in the Fall of 2008," *Investopedia,* May 8, 2017. http://www.investopedia.com/articles/economics/09/subprime-market-2008.asp. Retrieved June 16, 2017.

policies may affect the financial health of major U.S. corporations, and therefore your personal job security or the value of personal stock investments.

You can't know how weather and other natural phenomena will affect your life. You can't know when a disaster such as a hurricane, tornado, earthquake, flood, or fire will threaten your personal safety, your home, or your job. In October 2012, Hurricane Sandy battered a 600-mile swath of the northeastern U.S. coast, causing more than $50 billion dollars in damage to homes and businesses. Sandy caused 157 deaths and left 8 million people without electricity for days or weeks. Businesses, hospitals, and public transportation were closed or disrupted, and many people suffered significant lost income. In January 2016 the "storm of the century" hit the U.S. east coast, resulting in $3 billion in economic losses, according to Moody's Analytics researchers.[4] In October 2016, Hurricane Matthew caused at least $6 billion in U.S. property damage alone, with a much higher toll when one includes the economic impact of business disruption. In advance of Hurricane Matthew, our colleague Kathy Jordan was forced to evacuate her home on Anastasia Island just south of Saint Augustine, Florida. Kathy left the island feeling it was a "just-in-case" scenario. Late in the night before landfall was expected, the National Weather Service predicted that Hurricane Matthew would flatten the island. Miraculously, the storm made a last-minute turn to the east, which kept the eye of the storm 30 miles offshore. Kathy's neighborhood suffered minimal damages despite peak 120-mile-per-hour winds. However, nearby areas on the island were devastated by flooding from the storm surge. As of July 2017, nine months after Matthew's unwelcome visit, many Anastasia Island residents were still trying to rebuild and recover from the hurricane. Kathy has flood insurance, but she knows that most of her neighbors do not, since their houses are set one foot above the elevation that triggers mortgage lenders' requirement for flood insurance. Kathy's perspective has always been that flood insurance is cheap compared with the cost of repairing damage caused by storm surge waters.

---

[4]Andrew Soergel, "'Storm of the Century' Heaps Billions in Losses on Local Economies," *US News and World Report,* January 26, 2016, https://www.usnews.com/news/articles/2016-01-26/storm-of-the-century-heaps-billions-in-losses-on-local-economies. Retrieved June 16, 2016.

She scratches her head when neighbors claim that while living one mile from the Atlantic Ocean and 11 feet above sea level, their homes are safe from flooding. Anyone who wants to roll the dice when it comes to property or flood insurance should consider this: 2016 featured 15 U.S. weather-related events that each resulted in at least $1 billion in economic losses. According to NOAA's National Centers for Environmental Information (NCEI):

> *The year 2016 was an unusual year, as there were 15 weather and climate events with losses exceeding $1 billion each across the United States. These events included drought, wildfire, 4 inland flood events, 8 severe storm events, and a tropical cyclone event. Cumulatively, these 15 events led to 138 fatalities and caused $46.0 billion in total, direct costs. The 2016 total was the second highest annual number of U.S. billion-dollar disasters, behind the 16 events that occurred in 2011.*[5]

NOAA may have classified 2016 as an "unusual year," but coming on the heels of 2011, which saw the costliest year ever of U.S. natural disasters, we think that preparing for the impact of natural disasters, via vehicles such as robust property and flood insurance, is a matter of common sense. Finally, while recognizing the economic impact of increasingly frequent natural disasters, we also must keep in mind the irreplaceable loss of life that accompanies them.

You can't know when your employment will be disrupted. You can't know whether your company may experience financial difficulties or be acquired by another business. You can't know whether your expertise will become outmoded or outsourced. You can't know when your company will decide to lay off employees, or whether your boss will decide you're not measuring up to his or her expectations.

Erin Wnorowski recently married co-author Ryan's close friend Pat McKenna. Erin is a talented healthcare administrator who is passionate about helping people improve their health and well-being. Pat is in graduate school studying Urban Planning, after having worked for a number of years in healthcare administration. For a year or so before their wedding date, Erin and Pat had budgeted for and planned their

---

[5] Adam B. Smith, "2016: A historic year for billion-dollar weather and climate disasters in U.S.," *NOAA Climate. Gov.*, January 9, 2017, https://www.climate.gov/news-features/blogs/beyond-data/2016-historic-year-billion-dollar-weather-and-climate-disasters-us. Retrieved June 16, 2017.

wedding. In alignment with the principle of responsibility, the couple decided that the expenses for the wedding should be their responsibility, not their parents'. So, they scoped their wedding expenses in a way that was affordable given Erin's salary and Pat's student status. Erin and Pat felt they had things under control. Then Erin was laid off from her job when the startup company she worked for fell on hard times. It was highly stressful for Erin to be out of work, especially at a time when she and Pat had higher expenses than usual. Erin recently started a new job. But with Pat in grad school, and Erin the sole breadwinner for the time being, they decided to economize by moving into a house with one of Pat's sisters.

You can't know when your life or that of a family member will experience challenges. No one knows when they or a family member will be struck with a serious illness or disability, or even death. You can't know when a new family member might be conceived and how expensive it will be to raise and educate that child or subsequent children. You can't know if your child might suffer from a learning disability or be blessed with one-of-a-kind talent, either of which might have financial implications. Nicolas Perez* and his former wife have two wonderful children, who are now grown and on their own. Nicolas never imagined he would get divorced. But after many years, sadly, his marriage was in ruins. He and his wife used a mediator to help with the divorce process, and to the credit of both parties, the breakup was respectful throughout. As everyone knows, divorce is a very expensive proposition. But because Nicolas prepared for the certainty of uncertainty, his financial situation has made the process much less stressful. Reflecting on the circumstances preceding and during his divorce, Nicolas said, "The cliché that money can't buy happiness is true. It didn't keep my marriage from breaking up. But because of my financial success, I realized it's not worth it to be unhappy. Financial success enabled me to leave."

So, What *Can* You Do About What You Can't Know?

Sometimes it may feel overwhelming to focus on the varied sources of uncertainty in our lives. In the short term, it may seem easier to avoid thinking about things that *might* happen to us that *might* cause us harm.

*This is a fictitious name of a real person who did not wish to be identified.

But, if we deny the certainty of uncertainty, most of us will at some point in our lives be faced with a stressful, perhaps even catastrophic, financial situation *that could have been avoided or mitigated.* Perhaps the triggering situation could not have been prevented, but the negative financial consequences surely could have been minimized.

What if, instead of burying your fear of those uncertain future events, you embraced the fact of uncertainty? What if you used the certainty of uncertainty as motivation to create financial security and independence for you and your loved ones?

If you are willing to "reframe" uncertainty from a negative to a positive, you can prepare yourself financially for the certainty of uncertainty using the Smart Money Philosophy, a method that co-author Doug developed over 30 years ago as a young financial advisor. Doug initially taught this financial planning model to his clients, and later to many of the 10,000 advisors he led as executive vice president of Advice and Retail Distribution for American Express Financial Advisors (now Ameriprise Financial). In the last 15 years, Doug and his colleagues at his company, think2perform, have taught this approach to countless financial advisors who have used it to help their clients reduce financial stress and meet their goals of financial security and independence.

The Smart Money Philosophy is based on the profound idea that the best way to prepare for the certainty of uncertainty is to organize your financial life so no matter what happens, you will be okay financially. When you follow the Smart Money Philosophy, you cover all your bases; so whenever you need money, you will have a smart place to get it.

KEY ELEMENTS OF THE SMART MONEY PHILOSOPHY

The Smart Money Philosophy offers a clear and simple framework for making financially smart decisions. The Smart Money Philosophy includes a step-by-step process for financial planning that you can use on your own or with the support of a financial advisor. Although applying the Smart Money Philosophy can involve the use of complex financial instruments, it does not require them. It will help you figure out basic strategies such as diversifying your investments and how to use financial products such as insurance. It guides you about what to do—or not do—when you need money. You can make your plan as complicated as your circumstances warrant, but the beauty of the Smart Money Philosophy is that you don't need to get involved in sophisticated investments or complicated wheeling-and-dealing to achieve and enjoy financial independence. The Smart Money Philosophy will help you put in place a powerful financial plan that includes three key elements: saving money, diversifying your assets, and managing uncertainty risks. That said, our experience has been that you can get the best results from using the Smart Money Philosophy if you enlist the support of a values-based financial advisor. We recommend you hire the right type of financial advisor to help you apply the Smart Money Philosophy. Such an advisor is not interested in directing you to investment products that maximize his or her profits. The right advisor for you is one who seeks to deeply understand and support your values and goals. The right advisor for you goes even beyond that. He or she encourages you on a continuous basis to keep engaged in key activities for financial, physical, and emotional goals you've prioritized. Though Donna Krone, whom you met in Chapter 3, left her 18-year practice as an AEFA financial advisor to pursue her passion to be a life coach, she and her husband greatly value the support their financial advisor provides, no more so than when Donna's husband recently began to contemplate retirement. As Donna said:

> We just had our financial planner come out to the house to help us plan for my husband's upcoming retirement. He asked a lot of questions about our values and goals, and really listened. I was so impressed with him. Usually when financial advisors ask questions about values and goals, it's to help them translate that information into the financial analysis. With our advisor, it was clear that he was asking about our plans, values, and goals because he was genuinely interested and wanted us to achieve our dreams.

Dennis and Diane Dykema, now happily retired, began their married life together in Iowa with very limited resources. Dennis became a college professor at Buena Vista College.[6] Diane was a real estate agent for four years, and after that worked at Buena Vista College as an administrator. In the early years of their marriage, Dennis and

---

[6]Buena Vista College became Buena Vista University in 1995.

Diane could never have imagined enjoying the financial security they treasure today. They credit their financial advisor with helping them develop a financial plan that incorporated Smart Money Philosophy principles. One of the best outcomes of their work with their advisor was ultimately to be able to buy a second home on fabled Sanibel Island off the Gulf coast of Florida. Their Sanibel Island home offers them and their family members extended periods of time when they can engage in outdoor fitness activities that contribute to their health and well-being. Following their financial plan over many years has also given Dennis and Diane the flexibility to provide financial help to children and grandchildren when needed.

Recognize That You Must Save Money

If you want to be certain you'll have enough money, you *must* save. *You must save money to have money.* There is no escaping that fundamental rule of the Smart Money Philosophy. You can never know with certainty that you won't need money. Therefore, there are no shortcuts to saving. If there is one lesson learned from the Great Recession that exploded in 2008–2009, it is this: You cannot rely on credit cards or home equity as sources of cash to make desired purchases. Before the housing bubble began to burst in 2006, many people mistakenly thought that they didn't have to save. Real estate values kept rising, and banks were often aggressive about offering home equity lines of credit (HELOCs) that made it easy for people to turn their home equity into cash. Then home property values deflated. Seven million Americans lost their homes to foreclosure during the Great Recession, and fewer than one-third of them are likely to ever buy a home again. As of the end of 2016, five million Americans—more than 10 percent of homeowners—still owed more on their homes than they are worth. Half of those held mortgages at least 20 percent more than their homes are worth.[7] A generation ago, people knew they had to save money and that they needed to keep on saving money, no matter their age. For example, Doug's dad grew up during the Great Depression. When he died in 2009 at age 84, he was

[7]Svenja Gudell, "Q4 2016 Negative Equity Report: Improvement Continues, But at a Much Slower Rate," *Zillow*, https://www.zillow.com/research/q4-2016-negative-equity-report-14393/, March 7, 2017. Retrieved on June 12, 2017.

still saving money. No matter what, find a way to spend less than you earn, so you can put money aside for future needs.

In addition to cultivating the habit of saving money yourself, make a point of encouraging children to save, even at a very young age. Erin and Doug Livermore have taught their five- and eight-year-old daughters to save at least half of the money received from doting grandparents and the cash they get from doing extra chores around the house. When five-year-old Addison broke the screen on her iPad, she had a smart place to go to pay for the repair—her piggy bank. As you can see, the Livermores are also teaching their kids the principle of responsibility. Making sure that teenagers learn how to manage and save money is one of the best gifts you can give them. Young adults can also benefit from their parents' encouragement to save. When Pat McKenna was in his mid-twenties and working as a healthcare administrator in a pediatric medical center, his mother encouraged him to open up an IRA. When Pat checked his IRA account balance only a few years later, he was surprised at how much its value had increased.

Put Your Investments in a Variety of Financial Instruments

Develop the discipline of placing your money in varied places, such as cash or cash equivalents i.e., a bank savings account, money market account, and CDs (certificates of deposit). Also diversify by putting some of your money in equity investments, such as stocks or real estate; fixed-income investments (government or corporate bonds); or insurance, such as life insurance, disability insurance, or long-term care insurance. When you establish your investment routines, make sure that the places to which you allocate investments are diversified. Having money in different places ensures that whenever you need money, and for whatever reason, you will have a smart place to get it. That also implies that you should put money away in instruments that have minimal or no risk, such as money market funds. You can also systematically buy government bonds, which are guaranteed by the government that issues them. Even in difficult economic times, it is unlikely that the U.S. government is going to go out of business.

To invest for retirement, you can also regularly put money into a tax-deferred retirement plan such as a company-sponsored 401(k), an IRA (individual retirement account), or tax-deferred annuity.

To prepare for the "certainty" of your children's college expenses, you can also set up special college savings plans (so-called "529 Plans") that include mutual funds. In addition, you can buy stocks, bonds, or mutual funds outside of any special plan for retirement or college savings.

When making decisions about how to save and invest your money, avoid the temptation to put all your money in any financial instrument that is currently performing at a high level, for example, a top-performing mutual fund or a real estate investment in a hot market. As we're writing this in June 2017, many people are investing in the latest phenomenon—the digital currency Bitcoin, up more than 200 percent over a period of six months. One bitcoin investment vehicle, the Bitcoin Investment Trust, recently soared 1,600 percent in a single month. Many experts warn that Bitcoin is in a bubble and headed for a correction. Like Newton's apple, "What goes up, must come down." A high-performing fund this month can crash and burn next month. So, don't put all your eggs in one basket. This advice sounds like a no-brainer, but it bears repeating, since so many people are seduced by the prospect of making a lot of money in a short time.

Use Insurance to Transfer Some of the Risks of Uncertainty to Someone Else

Many of us make the mistake of "insuring the golden egg but not the income or life of the goose that laid the golden egg." In most states, you can't drive a car without car insurance. The simple idea everyone understands is that if you have a car accident, the costs of repairing vehicles and treating injuries can be enormous. The government therefore requires that we have a way to pay for those potential costs. But automobile insurance doesn't adequately insure the income or life of the person who drives or is a passenger in the insured car. It's ironic that we don't apply the simple logic of car insurance to other likely life events. Life crises can be massively expensive. That is why insurance is so important. When we buy insurance, we transfer some of the financial risks of uncertainty to others, that is, insurance companies.

- You don't know when you'll get sick or injured and need healthcare, but if you have health insurance, you can greatly reduce uncertainty about how much you would have to pay to get treatment for a major health problem.

- You don't know when you'll die, but you can transfer the financial risk of dying early to a life insurance company, thus providing funds to support your loved ones after your death.
- You don't know if an illness or injury will happen, but you can transfer the risk of being unable to work to an insurance company that offers disability insurance.
- You don't know if a disability will make it impossible to care for yourself, but it's highly likely, since 70 percent of people 65 or older will need some kind of care before death.[8] You can transfer the financial risk of needing care (for example, in an assisted living or nursing home) by using long-term care insurance.

Doug shares this example of what happens when you don't use the Smart Money Philosophy:

When my mom died, she didn't have life insurance. She was the only working spouse because my dad had previously retired, and her death produced both death expenses and resulted in lost income to the family. When my dad moved into an assisted living facility, he didn't have long-term care insurance, and had to pay for it out of pocket using his investments. Even if you enjoyed excellent returns on your lifetime investments, the costs of long-term care can wipe out your legacy. I was a CFP by the time my parents were getting older, and regret that I didn't help my parents recognize the importance of insurance.

Doug shares this example about how he used the Smart Money philosophy:

My son went to college at a time when the stock market had been on an upswing. Because my wife Beth Ann and I had invested in the stock market for years, we had a smart place to go for tuition money. We sold stocks whose value had gone up since we had bought them. When our oldest daughter started college in 2003, our stock investments had been pummeled. Had we sold stocks to pay for her tuition, we would have taken losses. But since we also had access to cash, we had a smart alternative: We paid her tuition in cash. When our younger daughter started college in 2006, stocks were up, so we sold profitable stocks to pay for her first two years of college. By my daughter's junior year, the stock market was dropping precipitously, so we paid her last two years of tuition by drawing on cash savings.

[8] "What Is Long-Term Care?" *NIH Senior Health*, https://nihseniorhealth.gov/longtermcare/whatislongtermcare/01.html.

MAKING YOUR OWN SMART MONEY PLAN

You already know that you're responsible for your financial well-being and that the best way to prepare for the certainty of uncertainty is to save and invest money. But how do you figure out how much you need to save? Ultimately the answer to that question is up to you. But we recommend that you aim for saving enough to be financially independent. Financial independence is sometimes thought of as freedom from the need to work. However, a more realistic definition is that financial independence is freedom from being financially dependent on anyone else. For some, financial independence can mean that you have enough income from your savings and other assets that you do not have to work, and that that income will come to you for as long as you need it. Another way to understand financial independence is to determine how much you need to "have enough" to align your day-to-day behavior with your values and goals.

Because you don't know with certainty how long you will need to have income, your plan for saving and accumulating assets ideally will be designed to keep generating adequate income indefinitely. We recognize that not everyone will be able to accomplish this goal. But even the act of setting financial goals, and taking steps to achieve them, will dramatically increase your financial security.

HOW MUCH DO YOU NEED?

How much you *really* need depends on how much income you think you need to support your desired lifestyle. What if someone said, "I will pay you enough money each month so you don't have to work ever again if you don't want to." How much would that be? For some people, the answer would be more than they make now. For others, it would be the same income they're making from their jobs. Still others would happily take, say, 60 percent of what they earn now if they could quit working—or change their behavior so they can financially support their values and key activities for their goals. Until five years ago, Brenda Blake was a successful, high-powered corporate executive with American Express. Today she is a vibrant yoga practitioner and founder of *Livin' Fully*, which offers programs that help women accelerate their personal and professional development. As Brenda explains on her website:

> *I had made a promise to myself a bunch of years back that I had to do or start something that gave me the flexibility to watch my boys play sports, to give myself at least an hour a day for my Yoga practice, the autonomy to be totally self-directed, and the opportunity to impact something that mattered.*[9]

So, when Brenda was 40 years old, she decided that she wanted to be able to leave corporate life and have the choice not to work by the time she was 50. Brenda and her husband put together a savings and investment plan that would allow her to do that. Brenda is now "livin' fully" in alignment with her values, and making a difference to the many women whose lives she touches through her organization's unique and powerful workshops and personal coaching. Another benefit of Brenda's current lifestyle is that she now has the freedom to spend four to five months a year in Tamarindo, on Costa Rica's Nicoya Peninsula, one of the five famous "Blue Zones" on Earth where people are healthiest and live the longest.

How much is enough for you? Do you want or need to replace all the income you are currently making in your job? Do you think you would be happy with less? Do you want more income than you currently make in salary to achieve your goals?

Saša Mirković immigrated to the United States in 1997 with only a suitcase and $1,400, which he had saved for an engagement ring for his then-fiancée Laura. When Saša told Laura about the money for the ring, Laura said, "I don't want to spend that much on a ring because that's like what it would cost to buy a sofa." Saša recalls that at that moment, he looked up to the sky and said to himself, "Thank you, God. We're going to be millionaires someday, because we agree about money." Saša and Laura found a less expensive ring and spent the rest of the money on two air-conditioning units that would get them through a hot and sticky Baltimore summer on the top-floor apartment of a converted townhouse on historic Charles Street. As a young married couple, Laura

[9]Brenda Blake. "Background," LivinFully.com, http://www.livinfully.com/background.html.

and Saša followed the Smart Money philosophy, and today they are financially very well off. Part of their secret is that they understand the concept of sufficiency—Saša describes Laura and himself as "delayed gratification people." They don't have any desire to keep up with the Joneses. They own a modest home in a good neighborhood. The money they don't spend on a McMansion goes to providing meaningful experiences and a healthy lifestyle for themselves and their three children. As Saša says, "To me, money is not a goal. Money and wealth are tools. The total dollar amount you have is irrelevant. It's what you use that money for."

SMART MONEY PLANNING GUIDELINES

Financial Aspirations. Smart money planning works backward. That is, it's helpful to decide how much money you need or want on an annual basis to accomplish your financial and personal goals, as Brenda Blake and her husband and Laura and Saša Mirković did.

Your next step is to begin a systematic savings and investment program based on the following planning framework:

- **Life includes two main events: your physical life and your death.** Your physical life ends when you die, but your financial life goes on beyond your death. That's because most of us leave behind some expenses, and often loved ones who need our financial support, or to whom we want to leave a financial legacy.
- **Health involves being healthy or not healthy.** Your health status may or may not affect your ability to work. Your health may affect your ability to generate desired levels of income.
- **The economy may be either strong or weak.** The strength of the economy can have varied effects on your financial status, depending on the particulars of economic conditions and your life, health, employment, and personal financial assets.

The Smart Money framework begins by systematically planning for worst-case scenarios related to life, health, and the economy before moving to more desirable life scenarios.

Smart Money Planning Scenarios

I. **Death.** Most people agree that untimely death is the worst-case scenario, both financially and personally. So, plan for death first. Determine, for instance, how much income or money your loved ones would need if you died suddenly. Then compare that with the income currently being generated by your existing capital and assets. If there is a gap, then buy enough life insurance to cover that gap. That ensures your family will have a smart place to get money in the event of your death.

II. **Life.** The financial needs you have during your physical life will vary depending on your health, your ability to work to gain income, and the varying nature of the economy. The major planning scenarios appear below:

  A. Not Healthy. A large percentage of people will experience the need for some significant medical treatment at some point in their lives. One trip to the emergency room with a child's broken bone can severely strain finances. That's why health insurance is so important. It's also very expensive, because so many people make claims against their health insurance. There are additional not-healthy scenarios that you need to plan for.

    1. Not Healthy and Not Able to Work: How much income would you need if you suddenly became unable to work? Compare that with the income you could generate from your existing capital and assets. If that is not sufficient to meet your needs, and even if it is, you should purchase long-term disability insurance.

    2. Not Healthy and Not Able to Care for Yourself: As you age, the risk of needing long-term care rises. According to one study, 37 percent of people who died at age 65 spent some time in a nursing home, while 71 percent of those who died at 95 years of age or older had spent time in a nursing home.[10] It's important to consider how you would

---

[10]"Health Aging Column—Long Term Care Insurance," *Colorado State University*, December 6, 2002, https://publicrelations.colostate.edu/2002/12/06/healthy-aging-column-long-term-care-insurance.

pay for nursing care, assisted living, or at-home healthcare if needed. All such care is expensive. Nearly one-fifth of people 65 and older will face these kinds of expenses before they die.[11] Even if you have enough reserve capital and assets to pay for such care, it's important to purchase long-term care insurance. Transferring the risk of a potential catastrophe to an insurance company is always a good idea. It is not a coincidence that the wealthiest people are the most well-insured.

B. Healthy.

1. **Planning for Difficult Times:** When the economy is weak or the markets are falling, it's important to have access to a variety of sources of funds, including instruments that perform well when the economy is struggling. These include cash, cash equivalents, fixed assets (instruments that have a fixed value such as a guaranteed annuity), fixed-income assets, and hard assets such as gold. You need a smart place to go for money to fund both positive and negative events, such as job loss, vacations, college tuition, and so on. Cash and cash equivalents may have changing interest rates, but the underlying value is fixed. Unlike cash, fixed-income investments, such as corporate, municipal, or government bonds, will have fluctuating value, but the income is fixed and therefore will continue to provide a specific amount of income no matter what is going on in the economy. Cash is especially useful for immediate needs, because it's available without penalty. Fixed-income investments are useful because by definition they provide a fixed income. Precious metals such as gold and silver can also be a smart place to get money during bad times. As we saw in the last decade, investments in precious metals often perform well when other investments, such as stocks or real estate, are declining. Figuring out how much of your total assets should be in cash and fixed-income instruments is both an art and a science. The concept is straightforward, but the nuances can be complicated. If you are a highly

---

[11] Family Caregiver Alliance, National Center on Caregiving, "Selected Long Term Care Statistics," https://www.caregiver.org/selected-long-term-care-statistics.

knowledgeable investor using the Smart Money Philosophy, you can accomplish a lot on your own. But most smart investors don't go it alone. They rely on financial advisors to help them identify and evaluate sophisticated options that will protect them during poor economic times.

2. **Planning for Good Times.** When the economy is strong, equity instruments such as company stocks and mutual funds of stocks tend to increase substantially in value. Participating in the stock market can help you reach financial independence more quickly, because on average over time, stocks perform better than fixed instruments such as bank CDs or government bonds. If you need money when the economy is strong, then selling equity assets that have appreciated is a smart way to get it. Like stocks, real estate investments are also equity investments, and depending on the nature of the investment, one might earn rental income or capital appreciation in those times when real estate values are rising. Someone once said, "We can't create more land, but we are adding more people, so it stands to reason that over time real estate is an asset that will appreciate."

ADJUSTING YOUR SMART MONEY PLAN

As you continue to save and invest money, you may need less coverage in some insurance plans than you did earlier. At that point you may discover that, even if you could get by with less insurance, reducing your level of coverage may not be a smart financial move. Continuing to use insurance to transfer risk to someone else can be less expensive than shouldering the risk completely yourself (even if you can afford to do so). Every year or so, review your financial picture, ideally with an advisor, and determine whether anything has changed significantly enough that you want to adjust either your goals or actions. This process should always be done while considering your values. When Doug was in his twenties, he calculated that he could be financially independent given the then lavish sum of $15,000 a year. As his family grew and living costs rose, he increased the amount he determined he needed to be free from the need to work. Your needs and wants will probably change over time. You can always adjust any action. For instance, values that influenced Doug's insurance decisions over many years include *family*, *wisdom*, and *health*. Doug values family. He believes it's wise to be well insured, and because health is fragile he understands that he can't count on the good health he's enjoyed all these years.

* * * * * *

The year before Doug started his first job in the financial services industry in 1973, the Dow Jones Industrial Average (DJIA) closed above 1,000. In December of 1972, the DJIA closed at 1,020. No one could know then that it would be another 10 years before the Dow closed the year above 1,000. The next time the Dow closed the year above 1,000 was at the end of 1982 when it closed at 1,047. Of course, it was far from a straight line for the stock market to reach those additional 27 DJIA points. During the 10 years between 1972 and 1982, the stock market zigged and zagged. But those 10 years taught Doug, and others who followed the stock market, that you really can't predict what the market will do. In the years since the market bottomed out in 2009, the DJIA has certainly resembled a rollercoaster ride, even though the general direction of the DJIA in the last number of years has been remarkably positive.

Regardless of what year you read this book, your life will zig and zag, too, and you'll probably need money to help you manage those twists and turns. Creating a financial plan based on the Smart Money Philosophy is the best way to prepare for the certainty of uncertainty and thereby reduce financial stress. Reducing financial stress using the Smart Money Philosophy will do much more than improve your financial health. As we'll see in the next few chapters, following the Smart Money Philosophy will also set the stage for living a healthier and happier life.

CHAPTER FIVE

Health

The first wealth is health.

—Ralph Waldo Emerson

Todd and Nancy Stepniewski have been happily married for 32 years. They have three wonderful kids in their twenties, and own three homes. Their primary residence is on Long Island, New York, and they have alternate home bases in Manhattan and Naples, Florida. When Todd and Nancy were starting out and raising a young family, finances were tight. They never dreamed that the life they live today was even possible. But thanks to Todd's success in building his financial advisory practice and Nancy's unending belief in him and support of him, their circumstances changed.

For Todd and Nancy, having multiple homes is not about having "assets." One reason they've invested in multiple properties is to support their value of family happiness. They chose homes that would provide appealing family gathering places as their kids and their families grew and took root in various parts of the country. For instance, during the winter months in the northern United States, where the kids all live, what better way to entice their family to visit than to offer them a sunny Florida destination where everyone can relax and reconnect? Whether or not their kids are visiting, spending time at their home in Naples allows them to easily engage in various outdoor health-promoting activities, rather than spending too many dark winter months cooped up in their Long Island, New York, home. When summer returns, their Long Island home is the perfect warm-weather destination for the family.

While family values are key to Todd and Nancy's decision to have multiple homes, they also see their investment in various homes as essential to supporting their value of lifelong health and well-being. Though there are many indoor fitness facilities that offer health-promoting activities year-round throughout the United States, most people benefit greatly from being active outdoors. Being able to be outside breathing fresh air, connecting with nature, and soaking up natural Vitamin D from the sun all convey exceptional health benefits. Todd and Nancy have the good fortune and health advantages of enjoying the outdoor life year-round.

If you're wondering how Todd and Nancy's Manhattan home, surrounded by the "concrete jungle" of one of the world's largest cities, contributes to health, consider the research on the relationship between engagement with the arts and health outcomes. James Aw, chief medical officer of the Medcan Clinic, a leading private health clinic in Toronto, Canada, has scoured the medical research to understand the connection between arts engagement and health. Here are results of several relevant studies described in Dr. Av's words:

- One Swedish study followed more than 10,000 people over the course of 14 years. It found a relationship between longevity and the people who most visited the cinema, concerts, museums, or art exhibitions—although interestingly, no link existed between longevity and those who attended sporting events.
- A Norwegian researcher, Koenraad Cuypers, performed statistical analysis on the health data of 50,797 Norwegians collected as part of something called the Nord-Trøndelag Health Study. Participation in cultural activities was significantly associated with good health, good satisfaction with life, and low anxiety and depression scores in both genders, Cuypers found.

According to the Norwegian study, participation in culture was good for you, regardless of whether you consumed or created the culture. And the more culture, the better the study participants' health. Frequency of cultural activity was positively associated with good health, life satisfaction, decreased anxiety, and decreased amounts of depression.

Based on this research, Aw encourages his patients to promote their health by engaging in hobbies and interests. He especially encourages his patients to build their social network by viewing or engaging in artistic and cultural events and activities.[1]

Todd and Nancy Stepniewski's home in Manhattan is at the world epicenter of culture. They are surrounded by many of the most famous artistic and musical venues in the world. Todd and Nancy live in walking distance of the most pleasurable and health-promoting cultural experiences anywhere. Taking advantage of Manhattan's cultural riches is bound to increase the odds of healthy longevity (not to mention fun) for Todd, Nancy, and their brood.

In keeping with the theme of the interconnection between money, health, and happiness, Todd and Nancy's story demonstrates how financial resources can enhance access to health-promoting locations. In fact, Naples, the location of one of their homes, ranks as the top community for well-being on the Gallup-Healthways Well-Being Index.[2] But Todd and Nancy also feel fortunate that their financial resources allow them to support health in other ways. Nancy firmly believes that health is the foundation of quality of life. She can't even imagine life without being healthy. So, Nancy focuses heavily on nutrition as a way of keeping the couple as healthy as possible. Todd jokes, "If you came into our house, you would think you were in a health food store."

Todd and Nancy are at a stage of life when health is a prime precondition for living a fulfilling life. All the Boomers interviewed for this

[1]James Aw, "Art for Life's Sake: The Health Benefits of Culture." *National Post*, August 32, 2011, http://nationalpost.com/health/art-for-lifes-sake-the-health-benefits-of-culture/wcm/852da57d-de01-4b2d-bab0-f1488490e67f.
[2]Dan Witters, "Naples, Florida, Remains Top US Metro for Well-Being," *Gallup*, March 7, 2017, http://www.gallup.com/poll/204536/naples-florida-remains-top-metro.aspx.

book emphasized the importance of health as they anticipated getting older. Fifty-something life coach Donna Krone noted that one of her top goals is to maintain her health. Donna says, "If you don't have your health, it's more challenging to feel fulfilled and happy." Michelle Arpin Begina says that her weekly exercise regimen is "non-negotiable." It wasn't always that way. When Michelle was younger, she struggled with her weight. "I had a relationship with sugar," recalls Michelle, "and I would gain weight and lose weight. I eventually decided to eliminate sugar and exercise regularly. I now plan what I eat and exercise four times a week." Michelle's personal objective is to die of old age, not from complications of diabetes or some other disease.

Marjorie Wynn deeply values her relationships with family and friends, and recognizes that health is connected to her ability to live out that value. As Marjorie points out, "If I'm not physically healthy, I won't be able to do many of the things I enjoy with those I love. It would also likely limit my ability to provide for my family. Without good health, everything else would be sub-par." Marjorie's husband, John, admits he sometimes takes his good health for granted. John enjoys being active. "I love to fix things," he says. "I love to build things, and help others with projects. If I couldn't do those things, it would be a big deal."

GenXer Laura Mirković discovered how vital good health was when she suffered hormonal imbalances related to the births of her children. Laura needed medication that, while solving some problems, caused unpleasant side effects. She discovered that the only way to get off meds was to exercise vigorously. Laura has been doing CrossFit[3] for 10 years, practices yoga, and enjoys biking. Laura's dedication to fitness has been a lifesaver. It keeps her grounded and energetic and allows her to be a great mom. Laura smiles when she says, "Everybody in the family knows I *need* to work out every day." Laura calls herself "the fitness leader" in the family, encouraging everyone, including her husband and three children, to stay active and make healthy choices. Part of Laura's motivation is watching her own mother, now in her eighties, unable to get around because she never moved enough when younger.

According to Laura's husband, Saša, "We look at fitness and healthy eating just like professional athletes do—as essential to our well-being

---

[3]CrossFit is a branded fitness program of high-intensity varied functional movements based in gymnastics, weightlifting, running, rowing, and other sports, https://www.crossfit.com/what-is-crossfit.

and success." Being financially secure makes their emphasis on health and fitness that much easier. Laura explains:

A lot of people in the United States have inexpensive gym memberships. Maybe they go; maybe they don't go. If you are only spending a little money, you don't have a lot of skin in the game. No one is checking in on you. I go to a CrossFit gym that costs $200 a month. I pay the extra money to go to CrossFit because it helps me with accountability for maintaining fitness. I get to work out with the same group of people every day. If I don't show up, someone calls me. I also have food buddies. If my food isn't in check, I can lean on a friend to support me in keeping my diet healthy. Saša and I believe if you buy cheap stuff or only invest a little bit, you'll end up spending more money in the long run or you'll develop medical issues. For example, if you're overweight, you're likely to end up needing a knee replacement.

Saša adds, "That's why I see a personal trainer several days a week at a cost of $500 a month, because for me to work out I need to have someone hold me accountable. I need a coach."

It's not just Boomers and mid-lifers who recognize the importance of health and health-promoting activities. Multiple surveys show that Millennials (born roughly between 1982 and 1996[4]) top the charts relative to older generations in their concern about health and wellness. Co-author Ryan, in his late twenties, starts his commute an hour early so he can work out at the office fitness center because he values the energy he gets from being fit. Thirty-four-year-old Erin Livermore heads out the door five times a week for her 6:00 AM Barre class because it sets the stage for a productive and happy day—no matter how stressful that day's job challenges may be. A 2015 Yahoo health study revealed these facts about Millennials' relationship to health:

- Millennials value health above everything except for family.
- Almost half of Millennials think of healthy eating as a continuing lifestyle choice rather than a time-limited diet.
- 84 percent of Millennials exercise at least once a week, and almost half think of exercise as their "passion."

[4]Manpower Group defines those born between 1982 and 1996 as Millennials. Goldman Sachs uses a broader range of those born between 1980 and 2000. Other organizations use similar but not identical age ranges.

- Though Millennials earn less than older generations, they spend more on health and fitness.
- Millennials are more likely to practice yoga and meditation and use natural treatments than older generations.
- 90 percent of Millennials seek to achieve good health because they believe it will help them succeed in other areas of life.[5]

As we follow Millennials in the years ahead, we hope that this upcoming generation will lead the way in reversing current negative public health trends. Millennials' appreciation of health and fitness may also become part of the solution to the U.S. healthcare crisis. As noted in a 2011 *New York Times* article:

> For the first time in history, lifestyle diseases like diabetes, heart disease, some cancers and others kill more people than communicable ones. Treating these diseases—and futile attempts to "cure them"—costs a fortune, more than one-seventh of our [U.S.] GDP.[6]

With statistics like that, it's no wonder that Reed Tuckson, author of *The Doctor in the Mirror*, emphasizes that doing what you can to be healthy is patriotic:

> If you want to do something for your country, for yourself, and for your grandchildren, turn off the TV and walk around the block a few times each day. Cut that bowl of ice cream in half. Get out and be active in the community.... Those are things you can control. That's being healthy. That's being patriotic.[7]

By taking responsibility for their personal health, Millennials may very well lead the charge in years ahead to reduce such massive and unsustainable medical care expenditures.

---

[5]Ann D'Adamo, "The Millennial Approach to Health & Wellness: 10 Amazing Facts," *Women's Marketing*, September 30, 2015, http://www.womensmarketing.com/blog/2015/09/the-millennial-approach-to-health-wellness/.
[6]Mark Bittner, "How to Save a Trillion Dollars," *New York Times*, April 12, 2011, https://opinionator.blogs.nytimes.com/2011/04/12/how-to-save-a-trillion-dollars/?_r=0. Retrieved May 1, 2017.
[7]Reed Tuckson, *The Doctor in the Mirror: Living a Longer, Healthier, More Joyful Life Starts with You*, United Health Services, 2011.

Like Todd and Nancy, Laura and Saša, Michelle, and Ryan, most of us strongly value our health—at least we *say* we do. Unlike the role models we interviewed for this book, many people don't translate their concern about good health into action. According to a 2015 survey on food and health,[8] almost everyone thinks about whether they are eating healthfully (91 percent) or getting enough physical activity (94 percent.) However, just over half of Americans (55 to 57 percent) actually take steps to maintain or improve their health, and that percentage has dropped dramatically in the last several years.[9]

What accounts for the disconnect between thinking about our health and acting to protect it? Some of us may be in denial about the need to be proactive about health. For instance, while most Americans (84 percent) think they are in good health, more than half of Americans who say they are in "very good" or "excellent" health are in fact overweight or obese.[10] More than a third of Americans blame a lack of willpower for their failure to engage in health-promoting habits. Others cite lack of time or money. But it's often a matter of priorities. We usually make time for things that we want to do: Nearly half of men who participated in the 2015 Food and Health Survey admitted that they spend more time following their favorite sport or team than tracking their diet.

BEING RESPONSIBLE FOR OUR HEALTH

An important part of the alignment model discussed in Chapter 2 is that we not only value health, but we accept the principle of responsibility for our health. Reed Tuckson, a traditional Western medical doctor, believes that much of our wellness is in our own hands. His book, *The Doctor in the Mirror*, is meant to convey the importance of being responsible for our health. The major message of Tuckson's book is that people who take responsibility for their health are healthier

[8] 2015 Food and Health Survey, International Food Information Council Foundation, http:// www.foodinsight.org/sites/default/files/2015%20Food%20And%20Health%20Survey-%20Executive%20Summary%20-%20Final.pdf. Retrieved April 25, 2017.
[9] Ibid.
[10] Ibid.

than people who leave responsibility for their health only to a doctor. As Tuckson points out:

> *No one knows what's going on inside your body like you do. And no one knows what's on your mind like you do, either. So, given the proper assistance, who do you think is eminently qualified to be one of your key health advisors? Just look in the mirror. You'll be face to face with one of the most capable doctors you've ever met. You'll be looking at the amazing, the brilliant, the esteemed Dr. You.*[11]

Tuckson wisely defines health broadly, not simply as the absence of pain or disease, but in a holistic way as a person's complete mental, physical, and spiritual well-being. Clearly Tuckson understands the connection between health and happiness, and we recommend his book highly for its valuable advice on key areas that affect your health—your lifestyle (such as nutrition and fitness), your medical needs, and your home and family.

Another way to be responsible for your health is to seek out a variety of qualified health advisors in addition to traditional practitioners of Western medicine. Alternative practitioners can provide perspective and guidance as you work to maintain and improve your health. For example, co-author Doug and his wife, Beth Ann, rely on their chiropractor, Dr. Moe Smith, for her guidance on positive health practices. She helps them identify the positive things they can to do to prevent illness, including guidance on nutrition, which their family doctor never discusses. According to Dr. Moe, chiropractic medicine is the largest noninvasive, nondrug, nonsurgical healthcare method in the world. Dr. Moe's practice is based on this philosophy: "Your body has innate intelligence. You're meant to be healthy. You're not meant to be sick." Dr. Moe advocates "treatments" such as healthy nutrition that reduce or eliminate the need for prescription medications. Dr. Moe's reservations about reliance on drugs in traditional Western medicine are based on both personal and professional experience. When Dr. Moe was four or five years old, she had a lazy eye, and was prescribed a drug that almost killed her. Even more tragically, her younger brother

---

[11] Reed Tuckson, *The Doctor in the Mirror: Living a Longer, Healthier, More Joyful Life Starts with You*, United Health Services, 2011.

died from complications of multiple medications. From a professional perspective, Dr. Moe points out that drug interactions are the fourth leading cause of death in the United States.[12] According to Dr. Moe, "Medical doctors are some of the smartest people I know, but they are given only three options to help their patients: perform surgery, prescribe medications, or do nothing."

We believe that medical doctors and traditional medicine contribute in important ways to our health and longevity. There are many circumstances in which medication or surgery are lifesaving. We always suggest you consult with a medical doctor whenever you have concerning symptoms. However, we do encourage you to consider seeking support from reputable natural health professionals, such as chiropractors, naturopaths, nutritionists, massage therapists, personal fitness trainers, and health coaches, who can support you in carrying out plans to maintain or improve your health.

WHAT DO YOU WANT FOR YOUR HEALTH?

As the research shows, developing health habits that contribute to your overall well-being is not an easy task for many of us. That's why WDYWFY is such an important tool for protecting your health. WDYWFY's Five Profoundly Simple Steps will help you take control of your health by turning desires for good health into realistic goals that pass the acid test. WDYWFY will help you develop and implement a solid and achievable health plan. One of the most valuable benefits of WDYWFY is that it allows you to track progress toward achieving better health and overcoming the disruptive emotions that are at the root of "lack of willpower." Everyone has their own health needs and desires. Some threats to our health are widespread in the United States, such as being overweight, poor diet, or smoking. To help you prioritize and achieve your health goals, begin by reading through the next section on common health issues. Also review recommended ways to address the most common health problems, since such ideas can help you adopt key activities for achieving your health goals.

[12]U.S. Food and Drug Administration, "Preventable Adverse Drug Reactions: A Focus on Drug Interactions," https://www.fda.gov/drugs/developmentapprovalprocess/developmentresources/druginteractionslabeling/ucm110632.htm. Retrieved July 4, 2017.

STRESS

When it comes to protecting your health, setting a goal for managing stress should be part of nearly everyone's health plan. In the last chapter, we discussed strategies for reducing financial stress. Financial stress alone is virtually an epidemic, with nearly 75 percent of us experiencing some degree of financial stress. But your body doesn't care what's causing you stress, whether it's concern about finances, worry about a child's behavior, or frustration with rush-hour traffic. Your body just reacts. So, when you add up all the different life situations that can cause stress, there's a 100 percent chance you will need to deal with the physical and emotional effects of stress in your daily life. Your ability to prevent and manage the negative effects of stress may be the most important skill you can develop to live a long and healthy life.

Can Stress Be Good for You?

Stress can be positive or negative. A certain amount of stress is beneficial. For instance, being under stress can improve your memory or increase your productivity and energy. It can help you deal with positive life challenges such as getting a new job, getting married, or having a child. Stress can also help you fight off certain illnesses by prompting release of hormones that support your immune system. But frequent or long-term stress is a disaster waiting to happen. Vast amounts of medical research show that chronic stress can interfere with the proper functioning of every one of your body's processes, and that sets you up for numerous health problems ranging from heart disease to headaches, digestive issues, weight gain, and sleep disorders, to name only a few.

Reducing Stress

Dan Buettner, National Geographic fellow and author of *The Blue Zones: 9 Lessons for Living Longer from the People Who've Lived the Longest*,[13] told co-author Doug a few years ago, "It's hard to be happy if you're not in good health."[14] And as we've seen, it's hard to be

---

[13] Dan Buettner, *The Blue Zones: 9 Lessons for Living Longer from the People Who've Lived the Longest*, 2nd Edition, National Geographic Partners LLC, 2011.
[14] Conversation between Dan Buettner and co-author, Doug Lennick, May 21, 2013.

healthy when you're under a lot of stress. When Dan studied regions all over the world whose residents enjoyed the longest and healthiest lives, chronic stress seemed noticeably absent. It's not that these remarkable Blue Zone 90- and 100-year-olds had never experienced hardship. In fact, many of them lived through horrendous conditions during World War II, when food was scarce and their lives were in constant danger. However, they all had developed practices to either eliminate sources of stress or at a minimum counteract a stressor's negative effects.

If you have started using the Smart Money Philosophy discussed in Chapter 3, you're already doing your body a favor by reducing financial stress. Of course, there are many other areas of life that can be stressful. So, whether you're worried about money, your kids, your job, or your health, excessive stress is generally bad for your physical and emotional well-being. Eliminating situations that trigger the stress response is the most direct and effective way to ward off the negative effects of stress.

Use Money to Reduce Stress

If your financial resources are sufficient, you can often use money to help remove or minimize causes of stress in nonfinancial areas of your life.

Several years ago, Erin and Doug Livermore's then four-year-old daughter, Addie, was expelled from two day care centers within three months. Addie had raging ADHD (attention-deficit hyperactivity disorder) and her behavior, such as running out of the school, throwing tantrums, or hitting other children, had become too dangerous. Addie was as difficult at home as she was at school. Erin and Doug tried to be patient, but weren't always successful. When Addie was expelled the second time, Erin and Doug were already slogging through the costly and sluggish bureaucratic process of having Addie's condition evaluated and her educational and medical needs determined. Meanwhile, as a two-career couple, they had to find quality care for a very difficult child. They knew there were long waiting lists for other day care centers, and that no day care center would be able to keep Addie even if they had an opening. They also realized that no ordinary babysitter could give Addie the structure she needed, and no ordinary babysitter would last more than a day with Addie.

Erin wanted to quit her job, but losing all her income wasn't practical in the costly Washington, DC, metropolitan area where they lived. So, Erin and Doug began their search for a nanny who had experience dealing with ADHD children. Miraculously, they found a wonderful, compassionate young woman who had grown up with a younger brother with severe ADHD. Their nanny now cares for Addie and Addie's older sister, Mackenzie, who is on the autism spectrum. Their nanny has been a one-woman stress reducer, but it has come at a price. Between the nanny's weekly salary and payroll taxes, Erin spends more than half of her gross salary on child care. But Erin and Doug think it's more than worth it. Their kids are happier. Erin and Doug are happier. They have backup on snow days, when kids are sick, and when they need to work later than usual. To further reduce their child care–related stress, and hopefully encourage their nanny to stay long term, Erin and Doug made a strategic decision when they first hired their nanny: They decided to pay her for the hours the kids were in school. That meant that their nanny would usually have at least three child-free paid hours per day when she was free to work on her online college studies or do whatever else she wanted. Erin and Doug valued flexibility, so they paid for it. In return, they got their nanny's loyalty and greatly minimized their child care stress. Today, both girls are doing well, in no small part a result of the loving and relaxing environment provided by their nanny.

Erin and Doug are grateful they made the decisions they made several years ago about how to manage care for their wonderful though challenging special needs children. But they wouldn't have been able to afford a nanny if they had not both previously set and implemented financial goals to advance their careers. When Erin and Doug arrived in the DC area in 2014, they both got jobs, but their combined income barely met their basic needs (even pre-nanny). Doug set a goal of increasing his income to a certain specified amount, and managed to reach his income goal by leveraging networking to find successively higher paying jobs three times within two years. In that same two years, Erin went from a below-market income as an accountant in a media company to a senior controller position, doubling her initial salary, primarily by working tirelessly and proactively taking on responsibilities well beyond her job level. Doug and Erin knew they needed to boost their income to get out of survival mode in the DC area, and they have succeeded.

Despite Doug and Erin Livermore's experience in achieving financial goals that in turn helped them manage stressful circumstances, neither would say that they've eliminated all the stress in their lives. When it comes to negative stress, there are some causes we can control. In many cases, we can't control or eliminate a source of stress, but we can always control how we react to stressful situations. We can always improve our ability to respond to life's trials in ways that keep stress from negatively affecting our physical and emotional well-being. Co-author Doug's belief is that reducing stress and maintaining one's physical and emotional equilibrium depends in large part on *preparation*. In Doug's view, preparation has four components:

1. Physical Preparation: Develop a "can-do" mindset. There is no substitute for doing, for taking action.
2. Mental Preparation: Whenever you say, "I'll cross that bridge when I come to it," realize that you should be mentally crossing it now.
3. Emotional Preparation: Anticipate the emotions you might experience when a stressful situation occurs and decide in advance how you will recognize and manage those emotions.
4. Moral Preparation: When dealing with stressful circumstances, avoid the temptation to ignore your principles. Ensure that your responses come from a place of integrity and are responsible and compassionate.

Stress Reduction Key Activities

In addition to the four components of preparation to manage negative stress, there are many useful life practices that can help you combat negative stress. According to the Mayo Clinic, effective stress management approaches include:[15]

- Eating a healthy diet
- Exercising regularly

[15]Mayo Clinic Staff, "Stress Relief," http://www.mayoclinic.org/healthy-lifestyle/stress-management/basics/stress-relief/hlv-20049495. Retrieved April 28, 2017.

- Getting enough sleep
- Making time for enjoyable activities (or as co-author Roy would say, "having fun!")
- Practicing meditation
- Seeking support from good friends or professional coaches or counselors

If stressful circumstances might be affecting the quality of your life—and that's the case for most of us to some degree—teach yourself the Mindful Breathing practice shown next. It's a surprisingly quick and effective way to immunize yourself from any negative physiological effects of stress.

PRACTICE: MINDFUL BREATHING[16]

A routine mindfulness practice can help you "retrain your brain" to be more resilient and better manage stress.

Use this quick meditation several times a day, or whenever you feel under pressure:

- Close your eyes for five minutes.
- Pay attention to your breathing, noticing how the air moves in and out of your nose.
- If your mind wanders, don't be concerned, just return to focusing on your breath as you inhale and exhale.

Tip: Decide on particular times when you will practice mindful breathing, for instance, when you wake up in the morning, before a meeting or presentation, before you walk in the house after a long work day, or after getting into bed for the night.

MANY DISEASES, ONE CURE

Our original intent was to provide readers with suggestions for key health-promoting activities that were tailored to readers' particular health concerns. We researched the most common life-limiting or

[16]Adapted from Jo Marchant, "Think Yourself Healthy," *Prevention Magazine*, January 2017.

life-threatening conditions, and investigated the best ways to prevent or manage top killer diseases. What we found should not have surprised us, but initially it did: Illnesses and disease conditions that could cause disability and limit life expectancy were varied. However, approaches to prevent or manage those varied diseases or conditions were virtually identical. Therefore, we first want to raise your awareness of the most common dangers to your health, most of which are caused by, and can be minimized by, lifestyle choices. We hope that this information will motivate you to set health goals and engage in key activities that can greatly lower your risk of disability or premature death. Nearly 75 percent of all deaths in the United States are attributed to just 10 causes, with the top three of these (heart disease, cancer, and stroke) accounting for over 50 percent of all deaths.

Heart Disease

Heart disease is the leading cause of death In the United States. That's true for both men and women. Women need to be especially mindful of heart disease risk, since most women think it's primarily a problem for men, not realizing that it's the most likely cause of death for women as well. One in three women who die each year die from heart disease, compared with 1 of 31 from breast cancer. Most women we know fear developing breast cancer, and it's a matter of frequent discussion among women, especially each time a friend is diagnosed with the disease. Women in our lives less often worry about heart disease or think to develop deliberate plans to minimize their risk of heart disease. In general, most people, men and women alike, dread the prospect of cancer. That said, as of 2017, heart disease still kills more people than all types of cancer combined.[17]

Cancer

According to the World Health Organization, cancer is the second leading cause of death globally, responsible for nearly one in six deaths

---

[17] Hannah K. Weir, PhD; Robert N. Anderson, PhD; Sallyann M. Coleman King, MD, MSc; Ashwini Soman, MPH; Trevor D. Thompson, BS; Yuling Hong, MD, MS, PhD; Bjorn Moller, PhD; Steven Leadbetter, MS, "Heart Disease and Cancer Deaths—Trends and Projections in the United States, 1969–2020," *CME ACTIVITY*, Volume 13, November 17, 2016, https://www.cdc.gov/pcd/issues/2016/16_0211.htm.

worldwide. In 2015, 8.8 million people died from cancer.[18] One-third of deaths from cancer are related to five lifestyle factors: high body mass index, low fruit and vegetable intake, lack of physical activity, tobacco use, and alcohol use. The cancer most responsible for cancer deaths in both men and women is lung cancer. According to the Mayo Clinic, women are also affected greatly by breast and colorectal cancers.

Stroke

Stroke is the second leading cause of death in women, and the fourth leading cause of death in men. Stroke risk factors are closely associated with heart disease. As research about cardiovascular disease has progressed, it has become clearer that the causes of heart disease and stroke are highly interconnected. For instance, plaque in arteries can result in a heart attack or a stroke, depending on the location of arterial blockages. So, though certain disease conditions may result in different symptoms, the causes may be the same.

Respiratory Diseases

Respiratory diseases such as chronic bronchitis and emphysema belong to a class of diseases called COPD, or chronic obstructive pulmonary disease. When combined, respiratory diseases represent the third largest cause of death in the United States. A large percentage of people don't realize they are suffering from respiratory diseases. The National Heart, Lung and Blood Institute recommends quitting smoking to prevent COPD, as it is the largest risk factor for chronic respiratory diseases.

Alzheimer's Disease

Alzheimer's disease is the fifth-leading cause of death in women, and the tenth in men. Alzheimer's is a form of dementia, characterized by progressive memory loss and inability to perform cognitive tasks, therefore interfering with normal daily life. Alzheimer's disease accounts for 60 to 80 percent of dementia cases. Doctors do not know exactly what causes Alzheimer's disease, but there may be a link between this disease and heart disease, as well as with head injuries.

[18]World Health Organization, "Cancer Fact Sheet," February 2017, http://www.who.int/ mediacentre/factsheets/fs297/en. Retrieved July 4, 2017.

Diabetes

Diabetes is commonly ranked as the seventh leading cause of death in the United States, though a recent study suggests that diabetes' contribution to deaths in the United States may be substantially underestimated.[19] Diabetes interferes with the body's ability to properly use blood sugar (glucose). Glucose is essential to health because it provides energy for all the cells in the body, including the brain.

When you have diabetes, you have too much glucose in your blood and that can lead to serious health problems that affect organ systems such as your heart and kidneys. It can also damage your nerves and blood vessels and can even cause blindness.

PREVENTING AND MANAGING THE MOST COMMON DISEASES

Whether you are concerned about conditions such as heart disease, cancer, diabetes, or Alzheimer's disease, research shows that there are steps you can take to minimize the likelihood that you will suffer from these serious health conditions. It's tempting to think that as you age, you are at the mercy of disease, especially if you have a family history of a condition such as heart disease or Alzheimer's. However, as Reed Tuckson, author of *The Doctor in the Mirror*, points out, "most of the deadly diseases afflicting those 60-plus are a direct result of behavior." Tuckson adds:

> *Your response plays a critical role in your future. If you decide, "I was dealt a lousy hand of cards; I'm going to fold," your life will reflect that negative response. But if you decide to draw a few new cards, good things can happen.... The good news is that to an extraordinary degree, YOU have control over your health status.*[20]

Key Activities for Preventing and Managing Health Threats

Research confirms Tuckson's message that a variety of the most common or dangerous health conditions can be prevented or limited by a

[19] Andrew Stokes and Samuel H. Preston, "Deaths Attributable to Diabetes in the United States: Comparison of Data Sources and Estimation Approaches," *PLOS ONE*, January 25, 2017, http://journals.plos.org/plosone/article?id=10.1371/journal.pone.0170219. Retrieved June 19, 2017.
[20] Reed V. Tuckson, *The Doctor in the Mirror*, United Health Services, 2011.

surprisingly small but important set of behaviors. Let's take one simple health practice as an example:

Walking for 30 minutes a day.[21] This activity can produce the following benefits:

- Protect brain health; slow down onset and impact of Alzheimer's disease
- Reduce heart disease risk
- Lower high blood pressure
- Reduce diabetes symptoms and risk
- Reduce risk of developing cancer

Maintaining Physical Fitness

Walking is only one example of how physical activity can contribute to overall health and disease prevention. Movement is crucial to maintaining a healthy weight, which lowers risk of the most common life-limiting health conditions. In addition to the disease-preventive benefits of exercise, physical activity conveys other important benefits.

Physical Agility

Being agile, able to move easily, engage in enjoyable physical activities, and perform life-sustaining tasks are all important to our sense of well-being and independence. The value of physical agility may be more obvious in one's later years, when many people experience difficulties with mobility that limit their physical independence or enjoyment of life. Donna Krone echoed one of Laura Mirković's reasons why health and physical fitness are so important to her as an active middle-aged woman:

> *I drive every day to visit my mom who lives in a nursing home. The only reason she needs to be in a care facility is because she can't walk. She's not happy about her situation. All of us wish she didn't have to live in a nursing home. I want to do everything I can now to ensure that I'm active and independent for the rest of my life.*

[21] "Walk Your Way to Health," *Age UK*, http://www.ageuk.org.uk/health-wellbeing/keeping-fit/walk-your-way-to-health/how-walking-can-improve-your-health.

Michelle Young believes fitness is vital to her family's well-being:

I think health is one of the most important things. Tom and I spend a lot of time working out. We eat well. I have a trainer who comes to my home twice a week. We spend time and money on our health. It's definitely a focus for us. It makes a difference in every dimension of life.

Michelle's husband, Tom, agrees with Michelle's emphasis on fitness:

I didn't exercise enough in my twenties but sometime in my thirties that changed. I work out 30 to 40 minutes every day. I get up at 5:00 or 5:15 in the morning to get my workouts in.

In *The Blue Zones*, Dan Buettner noted that the older people he studied in global regions with the greatest longevity were unusually active, compared with our U.S. stereotypes about capacities of older people. For example, Buettner describes his encounter in Sardinia with Torino, a 75-year-old shepherd:

When I caught up with Torino, he was slaughtering a cow in the shed behind his house. . . . It was 9:45 a.m. on a cool November morning. Torino had been up since 4 and had already pastured his sheep, cut wood, trimmed olive trees, fed his cows, and eviscerated this 18-month-old cow that was now hanging spread-eagle from the rafters.[22]

According to Torino's wife, he lives to work. Clearly, "retirement" is not in the Sardinian vocabulary.

In Okinawa, Buettner spent time with a centenarian woman living independently who easily sat down on the floor and just as fluidly stood up from the floor when needed. By the time we are in our forties, many of us in the United States grunt as we struggle to get up from sitting on the floor. Buettner took this lesson from his encounters with Okinawans:

Stay active.

Older Okinawans are active walkers and gardeners. The Okinawan household has very little furniture; residents take meals and relax sitting on tatami mats on the floor. The fact that old people get up and down

---

[22] Dan Buettner, *The Blue Zones: 9 Lessons for Living Longer from the People Who've Lived the Longest, 2nd Edition*. National Geographic Partners LLC, 2011, page 46.

off the floor several dozen times daily builds lower body strength and balance, which helps protect against dangerous falls.

Regular exercise does more than keep us physically fit. Harvard Medical School summarized a number of studies that demonstrate the positive effects of exercise on the brain:

Many studies have suggested that the parts of the brain that control thinking and memory (the prefrontal cortex and medial temporal cortex) have greater volume in people who exercise versus people who don't. "Even more exciting is the finding that engaging in a program of regular exercise of moderate intensity over six months or a year is associated with an increase in the volume of selected brain regions," says Dr. Scott McGinnis, a neurologist at Brigham and Women's Hospital and an instructor in neurology at Harvard Medical School.[23]

So, whether you're enjoying a brisk walk on the beach, working out on an elliptical machine, or racking up miles on a stationary bike, you're simultaneously achieving a healthy weight, lowering your risk of numerous diseases, and upping your IQ! As if those benefits weren't enough to get you moving, Dr. Tuckson suggests that being active gives our life purpose:

. . . being active entails much more than running around in a sweat suit flexing your muscles. Being active is how you fulfill your purpose in life. It's how you grow to become a "complete" person, actively sharing your talents with others.[24]

If you can't move, if you aren't active, it's a lot more challenging to accomplish other life goals, especially goals that involve serving others.

Finally, being active is closely connected to being happy. Sonja Lyubomirsky and other researchers have found that one of the characteristics of the happiest participants in their studies was that they make physical exercise a regular habit.[25]

---

[23] Heidi Goldman, "Regular exercise changes the brain to improve memory, thinking skills," Harvard Health Blog, Harvard Medical School, April 9, 2014, http://www.health.harvard.edu/blog/regular-exercise-changes-brain-improve-memory-thinking-skills-201404097110. Retrieved May 1, 2017.

[24] Reed V. Tuckson, *The Doctor in the Mirror*, United Health Services, 2011.

[25] Sonja Lyubomirsky, *The Myths of Happiness: What Should Make You Happy but Doesn't. What Shouldn't Make You Happy but Does*, New York: Penguin, 2014, page 23 (paperback).

EATING HEALTHFULLY

Maintaining a healthy weight is critical for overall health. Maintaining a healthy weight lowers the risk of developing the most common life-limiting diseases, including heart disease, stroke, diabetes, high blood pressure, and various types of cancer. In addition to health benefits, staying at a healthy weight has personal and social benefits. Most of us feel better about ourselves when we are at a normal weight. Our appeal to potential friends, romantic partners, or employers is often positively affected by maintaining an attractive, healthy weight. Most adults gain one or two pounds a year. That may not seem like much, but over the course of 10 or more years, a small yearly weight increase can result in a large health problem. Diet and exercise are the primary areas to focus on when you want to prevent weight gain or lose unhealthy weight. As we all know, there are countless dietary

F I G U R E   5 . 1   HEALTHY EATING PLATE

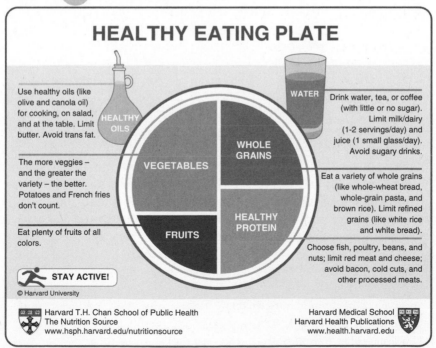

Source: Harvard T.H. Chan School of Public Health, The Nutrition Source.

regimens that claim to help maintain or lose weight: South Beach, Atkins, Weight Watchers, Nutrisystem, Paleo, Mediterranean, and many others. Though the ingredients may differ for each, they all have in common what one of the author's family doctor calls the "ELF" diet, which is short for "eat less food." So, a basic key activity for losing weight or preventing weight gain is to regulate calories so you don't eat more calories than you need to preserve your health and achieve your weight goals. By tracking your calorie intake and your weight over time, you'll be able to determine an ideal calorie range for you.

While the quantity of food you eat is important, another key activity is to pay attention to the quality of the foods you eat (Figure 5.1). Drinking a 120-calorie soft drink may have the same impact on your weight as a cup of 2 percent milk (also 120 calories), but the nutritional benefits of each could not be more different. Milk provides high-quality protein, vitamin A for immune system support, energizing B vitamins, calcium, and vitamin D to strengthen bones, as well as lower cancer and dementia risk. A soft drink provides a tempting sugar high, but offers no nutritional benefits. In fact, soft drinks significantly increase the risk of diabetes, heart disease, and other serious chronic conditions.

LUSTING AFTER LATE-NIGHT PIZZA

When co-author Doug is at home, he and his wife Beth Ann stay on a healthy eating regimen—eating early, eating lots of vegetables, and keeping food portions reasonable. But when traveling, it's a whole other story. On the road, Doug usually gets back to his hotel late after a long day of work and evening business networking. He's usually in a physically and emotionally weakened state by then and gravitates to comfort food, including his two favorites, pizza and bacon cheeseburgers. Doug is gradually learning how to overcome the temptation of unhealthy eating when traveling, including taking charge of his evening schedule so he can get back to his hotel earlier; or packing healthy snacks, such as nuts and dried fruit, that he can eat at the end of the work day so he isn't ravenous when he finally returns to his hotel room for the night.

PRIORITIZING YOUR HEALTH GOALS

In this chapter, we've explored the top health challenges that can affect your ability to live in alignment with principles and values. Though you can't control everything about your health, you can do much to improve your health. As we've seen, the diseases most likely to limit the quality and length of our lives are "lifestyle diseases"—caused in large part by our choices. We are responsible for leading the healthiest lives possible. No matter what stage of life you are in, or what state of health you are in, you can improve the quality of your life by adopting healthy living habits. And the best way to begin to improve your health

---

FITNESS TIPS

Try one or more of the following:

- **Find a fitness role model.** Look for stories online about interesting amateur athletes who keep fit with activities that you might enjoy. For example:
  - Tao Porchon-Lynch, at 98, the world's oldest yoga teacher[26]
  - Charles Eugster, who was at age 97 the world's oldest body builder (and only started training at age 87)[27]
  - Reflect on what attracts you to these individuals' stories. What about their lives inspires you? In what ways might you emulate them?
- **Reignite your passion** for an activity or sport that you used to engage in. For example:
  - Take a dance class.
  - Join a community softball team.
  - Raise money by participating in charity walks.
- **Get an exercise buddy**. For instance, find a friend or neighbor to join you on a daily walk, weekly tennis match, or working out with free weights.[28]

---

[26] Tao Porchon-Lynch, TaoPorchonLynch.com, http://www.taoporchon-lynch.com/.
[27] Sadie Nicholas, "Just a number: Meet the 97-year-old bodybuilder who refuses to retire," Sunday Express online, http://www.express.co.uk/entertainment/books/762775/bodybuilder-pensioner-retirement-age-just-number-book.
[28] Miriam Nelson's bestseller, *Strong Women Stay Young*, is an excellent guide to strength training for do-it yourselfers.

is to use the WDYWFY goal achievement model to envision, plan, and implement your health goals. WDYWFY, which lays out five simple steps for goal achievement, begins with "Have a goal." One way to hone in on important health goals is to visualize how you would like to be at your healthiest and fittest.

Identifying fitness role models can inspire you to adopt health-promoting habits you might not have otherwise imagined. For example, London-born Charles Eugster, who once practiced dentistry, was at one time probably the fittest senior citizen on the planet. At the age of 63, Charles took up competitive rowing for the first time since his college days. When rowing left him short of breath, he learned that he suffered from a heart arrhythmia. So, to keep fit, he switched to a less aerobic form of exercise. At 87, by now retired and widowed, Eugster hired a former Mr. Universe to coach him in body building. Sadly, as this book was being written, Charles Eugster died at 97 of complications following heart failure.[29],[30]

These stories of extraordinary later-life athletes are certainly inspiring. But they can also be intimidating. We might think we could never achieve their level of fitness, no matter what our age. However, most of us have someone in our lives, a friend or family member, who can serve as a role model for health. In co-author Doug's life, his role model is his wife. Beth Ann is in perfect health and her commitment to fitness is extraordinary. She exercises regularly and takes her yoga practice seriously. Beth Ann embraces healthy eating habits, including eating frequent, small amounts of healthy food four or five times a day. Beth Ann introduced Doug to kombucha, a fermented tea with many claimed health benefits including improved digestion and liver function, as well as overall immune system support. Beth Ann also introduced Doug to alternative healthcare professionals such as Dr. Moe, their chiropractor. Because of Beth Ann's influence, they avoid late night eating, and Doug has learned the benefits of eating breakfast (mixed fruit) and enjoying vegetables and salads as the foundation of other meals.

---

[29]Sadie Nicholas, "Just a number: Meet the 97-year-old bodybuilder who refuses to retire," Sunday Express online, http://www.express.co.uk/entertainment/books/762775/bodybuilder-pensioner-retirement-age-just-number-book.
[30]"Charles Eugster, "Elderly Bodybuilder and Athlete—Obituary," *The Telegraph*, May 2, 2017, http://www.telegraph.co.uk/obituaries/2017/05/02/charles-eugster-elderly-bodybuilder-athlete-obituary.

MAKE A PLAN FOR YOUR HEALTH GOALS

Once you've imagined yourself at your fit, active, and energetic best (your ideal health self), it's time to set goals that can help you move toward that healthy state. Keep in mind that no matter how young or old you are, you have the right and responsibility to work toward the healthiest and most vibrant life possible.

When you realize the impact of health-promoting activities on your overall well-being, it can be tempting to make a long list of health and fitness goals. That can be overwhelming. So, start with one simple goal. Maybe it's a goal to add more vegetables to your daily diet. Maybe it's a goal to add a physical activity to your schedule twice a week. Then use the worksheets, "Turning Wants into Goals" and "Goal Achievement," in Appendix E to map out the activities and resources you'll need to achieve your health goal. You can also download copies of these worksheets from the book Toolkit at www.leveragingfi.com.

BEYOND PHYSICAL HEALTH

When Brenda Blake was in her thirties, she and her family moved to Arizona. Brenda became part of a corporate culture that valued golf. Brenda enjoyed the game and being outdoors surrounded by beautiful scenery. But the combination of all that golf and being on the road traveling took its toll on her back. To help relieve her back pain, Brenda started taking a yoga class at her local community center. To her dismay, the yoga class was 90 minutes long. She felt guilty being away from her young sons for that long, and initially didn't understand the value of such a lengthy class. Brenda was also impatient with the meditative aspects of the yoga class, which made her feel sleepy. Brenda understandably wanted an efficient way to improve her back condition so she could keep playing golf. Basically, she wanted a physical solution to a physical problem. And though it was time-consuming, her yoga classes were improving her back condition. Then one day, Brenda decided to take a class at another location. At the end of the session, her teacher encouraged the class to go into a meditative state and just focus on who they were. "Wipe all the roles away—mother, wife, job," her teacher said. Brenda felt shocked because if she wasn't defined by her roles, she wasn't sure who she was. For Brenda, that was a turning point. She realized that yoga was not just about improving her physical condition. Yoga was a way to help her become all that she wanted to be, both physically and mentally. According to Brenda, "Many people go to yoga for physical reasons and then get addicted to it because it integrates mind/body benefits." Luckily, that was what happened for Brenda.

Brenda offers several important pieces of advice about promoting optimum health:

- First find an activity that engages you so you become "addicted" to it. For Brenda, yoga is one of her positive addictions.
- If you find yourself addicted to a physical activity, such as running, balance that by adding a mental practice, such as meditation.
- If you're addicted to a mental practice, such as meditation, balance that with a physical activity such as walking or strength training.

* * * * * *

In this chapter, we have focused primarily on practices to improve our health. As we stand at the intersection of money, health, and happiness, it's clear that every step we take to improve our physical health positively affects our financial and emotional health. In the next chapter, we'll complete the virtuous circle of money, health, and happiness. We'll introduce you to a number of effective steps to improve your overall well-being and happiness.

CHAPTER SIX

Happiness

Happiness is the meaning and the purpose of life, the whole aim and end of human existence.

—Aristotle

Jean and Howdy Mathiasen are wonderful, active newlyweds who both recently celebrated their eightieth birthdays. Everyone who knows them says that Jean and Howdy are the happiest couple they've ever seen. But life hasn't always been kind to them. Howdy's first wife died after a nine-year battle with cancer. Thirty years ago, in his late forties, Howdy suffered a serious stroke, which practically destroyed his short-term memory, and cost him his job as a successful bank executive. Howdy had always been a walker, but after his stroke, and living on disability income, he decided he should walk even more. He spent more time improving his golf game. Howdy also developed strategies to compensate for his poor memory, such as a notebook that he writes everything down in to remind him of what's happening and what needs to be done. Jean's first marriage was very troubled. She was a stay-at-home mom of three, who had to go back to work when her alcoholic husband became unable to support the family. Jean didn't make much money, so she had to be frugal. Jean's daughter, Caroline, recalls her mother's mantra when she was growing up—"Health Is Wealth." Caroline must have heard that a thousand times. Jean put a lot of emphasis on preparing nutritious meals for her family. According to Caroline, "My mom's idea of dessert was a homemade bran muffin." In those years, produce was cheaper than fast food, but for an occasional dinner, Jean would "treat" her kids with their favorite McDonald's hamburgers. If she had a little extra money, she'd splurge and buy them fries as well. Jean also stayed physically active. No matter how busy Jean was with work and kids, she found time every day for her walks. Jean's life circumstances were stressful, but she did everything she could to maintain her own and her children's health and well-being.

Today, Jean and Howdy, who first met in fourth grade, are an amazingly contented and joyful couple who give each other credit for their high level of happiness. Howdy says, "Jean makes me happy. As we've been together longer and longer, she makes me happier and happier. We like to do things together." Jean adds, "Howard is the most important part of my happiness. I always say that this is the happiest I've ever been in my life. We fit together well. We really appreciate each other. We were in our seventies when we got together so we appreciate every day. We appreciate feeling good." Most of their happiness doesn't come by accident. They walk together almost every day, chatting about whatever is on their minds while enjoying spectacular views of the Rocky Mountains that tower to the west of their suburban Denver townhome. Several times a week, they go to the gym to work out. Jean also practices yoga. And Howdy frequently plays golf. They socialize with friends, enjoying movie matinees followed by dinners full of laughter. They're learning new skills. Recently Jean, a talented pianist, started a bartering arrangement with a friend who is fluent in Spanish. Once a week, they get together. Jean gives her friend a half-hour piano lesson. Then her friend gives Jean and Howdy a half-hour Spanish lesson. Jean and Howdy don't have a lot of money. In fact, they recently had to get a line of credit to help pay for a new roof. But they don't feel financially stressed because they know how to pay off that debt no matter what the future holds. Jean and Howdy are wealthy in all the ways that count—they are together, they're financially stable, they have good friendships, and they're healthy. What a recipe for happiness!

FINDING YOUR HAPPINESS RECIPE

Sonja Lyubomirsky, a psychologist who studies happiness, has summarized all the research on factors that determine happiness. Fifty percent of our happiness is a matter of our genetics. It's true that each of us has an inborn happiness level. Some of us are naturally happier than others. Another 10 percent of our happiness is a function of life circumstances. That means that conditions related to finances, health, marital status, or career affect our happiness. But even when circumstances throw us off balance, we are never completely at their mercy. Why? Because 40 percent of our happiness is determined by how we *behave*.[1] We always have a choice about how to respond to life's challenges. We can behave in ways that make us miserable. But if we're wise, we can take action to restore or improve our happiness level. Co-author Doug was recently reminded of the power of behavior to affect personal well-being during a very difficult time in his family's life.

A few years ago, Doug found himself unexpectedly under stress because of a number of challenging family circumstances over the course of eight months. First came his daughter's divorce, which was heartbreaking not only because it was painful to watch his daughter suffer, but also because Doug's family considered her spouse part of the Lennick family, so it was a personal loss for him as well. Then his father-in-law ended up in a nursing home following a fall in his home that accelerated his dementia. Not long after, Doug turned 63, the age his mother had been when she died. Everyone who has reached the age of a parent's death knows how strange and sad that feels, though there is no good word to describe it. Then his son's father-in-law died, another painful event, even more so because of the closeness between the Lennicks and Doug's daughter-in-law's family. As much as Doug practiced self-awareness, he thought he was fine. He wasn't. Family is one of Doug's top values, and having so many tough life events happen to his family in such a short time rocked him emotionally.

In response to Doug's emotional stress, Doug's physical health began to deteriorate. He found himself eating more junk food, eventually gaining some unwanted extra weight. He managed to catch a case of poison ivy so severe that two doctors labeled it the worst case

[1] Sonja Lyubomirsky, *The How of Happiness: A New Approach to Getting the Life You Want* (New York: Penguin Books, 2007), pp. 20–22.

they'd ever seen. He had to take powerful steroid medication, which in turn gave him high blood pressure. So, Doug then had to take medication to lower his blood pressure. The worse he felt physically, the worse he felt emotionally. Doug found himself worrying, not just about his family's current problems, but also about other negative things that might happen. He started imagining his own worst-case scenarios: "What if I became incapacitated or died? Would there be enough money for medical expenses? Would Beth Ann be okay?" Even though Doug followed the Smart Money Philosophy, he still obsessed about the idea that something could happen which would threaten his family's financial security. Doug was unhappy, unhealthy, and on a few occasions uncharacteristically irritable. But Doug was fortunate to have the support of his wife, Beth Ann, his children, and even his son-in-law and daughter-in-law, who began to give him feedback about his mood and other unhealthy behaviors. Those were the wake-up calls that helped Doug get back on track. Doug amped up his workout schedule and revamped his diet. Doug also tackled the source of worry about his family's future. He wanted to make sure that no matter what happened to him, he and his wife Beth Ann would be financially secure. So, Doug met with his financial advisor to double-check that he was prepared for the certainty of uncertainty. Within six months or so, Doug's sense of well-being was restored to a great degree. Everything is not perfect for Doug's family. Like every family, they still have challenges. But Doug is back to his more typical happy self. He is relying on what Sonja Lyubomirsky calls "the 40 percent solution"[2]—the percentage of our happiness that we can control by our actions. In alignment model terms, Doug is using the WDYWFY goal achievement process to align his behavior with his values of family and happiness.

HAPPINESS IS MORE THAN A CHEERFUL MOOD

Martin Seligman is known as one of the founders of the "Positive Psychology" movement. For most of the history of the field of psychology, research was focused on helping people overcome "negative" mental states such as depression and anxiety. Seligman and his colleagues shook

[2]Sonja Lyubomirsky, *The How of Happiness: A New Approach to Getting the Life You Want* (New York: Penguin Books, 2007), p. 20.

up the psychology research community when they decided to focus their work on an area of inquiry that many skeptical psychologists didn't take seriously: understanding positive mental states such as happiness and developing tools to help people get more out of life. Seligman's original model was called "Authentic Happiness." According to Seligman, happiness includes three factors: positive emotion, engagement, and meaning. Positive emotion is the element that most of us think of as happiness—pleasure, excitement, contentment, and so on. The second factor, "engagement," is about the state you are in when fully absorbed in an activity, say playing a musical instrument, working on an art project, or running through the woods. Engagement isn't an emotional state at all. When fully engaged in something, you're not consciously aware of thinking or feeling anything—you just "are."[3] Engagement is similar to what psychologist Mihaly Csikszentmihalyi calls "flow."[4] It's a deeply satisfying experience that is impossible to describe using the vocabulary of emotions.

According to Seligman, the third aspect of happiness is meaning. Imagine if your definition of happiness included only the first two aspects of Seligman's Authentic Happiness model: You feel good and you have experiences of being totally engaged in desirable activities. Let's say you're generally enjoying your life, feeling enjoyment while travelling for pleasure or eating wonderful food at the latest destination restaurant, and you periodically engage in an activity, say a favorite video game, that puts you in a state of "flow" or complete absorption. Are these two elements, positive emotions and engagement, enough to give you true happiness? For most people, the answer is no. When it comes to happiness, we can "feel" good and we can be engaged in absorbing activities, but what if those pursuits are trivial? A great meal can delight us, and a video game can fully absorb us, but they are temporary experiences. True happiness comes from engaging in experiences that provide meaning. As Seligman points out:

Human beings, ineluctably, want meaning and purpose in life. The Meaningful Life consists in belonging to and serving something that you believe is bigger than the self, and humanity creates all the positive

[3] Martin E. P. Seligman, *Flourish* (New York: Atria, 2011), p 11.
[4] Mihaly Csikszentmihalyi, *Flow: The Psychology of Optimal Experience* (New York: Harper, 2008).

institutions to allow this: religion, political party, being green, the Boy Scouts, or the family.[5]

Richard Leider echoes Seligman's perspective on the connection between purpose and happiness. In one of his blog posts, Leider reminds us that "A sense of life purpose promotes physical, mental, and spiritual health. People who seek meaning beyond themselves are healthier, happier, and live longer."[6] Sonja Lyubomirsky, whose research on happiness we've referred to before, offers a similar point of view to that of Seligman and Leider. She uses the term *happiness* to refer to "the experience of joy, contentment, or positive well-being, combined with a sense that one's life is good, meaningful, and worthwhile." Lyubomirsky's research also confirms that working to achieve goals is an essential component of happiness.[7] Co-author Roy Geer, who developed the WDYWFY model for goal achievement 50 years ago, could not have agreed more with those findings.

HAPPINESS MEANS LIVING IN ALIGNMENT

Seligman's theory of Authentic Happiness, Leider's work on purpose, Lyubomirsky's definition of happiness, and co-author Roy Geer's insight about values-based goal achievement validate the idea that true happiness requires engaging in activities that are aligned with principles, values, and goals. The people we know or have worked with professionally who live the happiest lives are those who take action to live in alignment with principles and values, and who set and achieve goals that support principles and values. So, let's review some elements of the alignment model that can help you pursue true happiness.

Happiness and Principles

The first frame of the alignment model consists of principles and values. As mentioned earlier, numerous studies show that there is a set of principles that is part of the moral codes of all cultures throughout

---

[5] Martin E. P. Seligman, *Flourish* (New York: Atria, 2011), p. 12.
[6] Richard Leider, "The Power of Purposeful Aging," *Inventure and the Purpose Company*, June 1, 2017, http://richardleider.com/the-power-of-purposeful-aging/.
[7] Sonja Lyubomirsky, *The How of Happiness: A New Approach to Getting the Life You Want* (New York: Penguin Books, 2007), p. 67.

the world.[8] To have the best life possible, to be as happy as possible, we need to keep universal principles in mind and put them into practice. All four universal principles connect strongly to happiness:

- Integrity
- Responsibility
- Compassion
- Forgiveness

These principles are a result of both nature and nurture. They are rooted in our inborn disposition to be moral; they are activated primarily by learning. Much of that learning happens as children grow up when ideally the "Golden Rule" is taught by parents, teachers, and other caretakers. Our ability to live in alignment with principles also depends on lifelong "re-learning," that is, by engaging in regular practices that enhance our ability to apply principles to our everyday behavior.[9] Later in the chapter you'll find detailed descriptions of practices that allow you to deepen your ability to act in concert with principles, thereby increasing your level of happiness.

When it comes to happiness, each of these principles are important, but none more so than the principle of *responsibility*. As Martin Seligman notes, happiness depends on serving, that is, being responsible for the welfare of others. To fully serve others requires that we embrace other principles as well: We need to be *compassionate* to others; we need to actively care about others. To be happy also means we need to *forgive* others when they let us down. If we expect perfection from others or ourselves, we will always be disappointed, and we will always have excuses to abandon our commitment to serve them. When we forgive others, we do them a service. We give them another chance with us. But just as important, we serve ourselves, because our brain isn't wired to feel happy and miserable at the same time. When we forgive others, we feel happy because we have preserved our relationships with the people who help give our lives meaning and purpose.

---

[8] For example, research of noted anthropologist Donald E. Brown, as discussed in *Human Universals* (Philadelphia: Temple University Press), 1991.
[9] See Doug Lennick and Fred Kiel, *Moral Intelligence 2.0* (Upper Saddle River, New Jersey: Prentice Hall, 2011) for extensive discussion of connection between universal principles and effective behavior in organizational settings.

Happiness and Values

Happiness also depends on living in alignment with your values. Unlike principles, which are universal, values are a matter of personal choice. In Chapter 2 you had an opportunity to identify your top five values. Did you list happiness as one of your top values? Whether or not you listed happiness as one of your top values, the more you live in alignment with all of your values, the more likely you are to experience happiness. But you're even more likely to be happy if you consciously value happiness. When you decide happiness is important, you can plan to be happy. When you make happiness a key part of your ideal self, and set goals to increase your happiness, you're well on the way to making happiness a consistent part of your real self.

For co-author Doug, spending time with his family makes him happy. Doug's travel schedule keeps him away from his family more than he'd like. When he is in town, he likes to get home after work to spend time with Beth Ann. That's why he limits after-work gatherings to an hour. Several years ago, Doug lost a friend who was annoyed with him for being unwilling to stay out late with him. As the saying goes, "With friends like those. . . ." Friends worth having don't disregard your values. They support your alignment with values. Real friends want you to be happy.

Happiness and Behavior

Aristotle, the famed Greek philosopher from 300 BC, understood that happiness was a function of action. His views about happiness include the following:

> *Happiness is activity.*
> *Happiness is a sort of action.*
> *The activity of happiness must occupy an entire lifetime; for one swallow does not a summer make.*

What Aristotle meant when he spoke about action included everything in the third frame of the alignment model—Behavior. When you align your thoughts, emotions, and outward actions with principles and values, you increase your happiness, especially if you value happiness itself, because happiness comes from working to become your ideal self.

HAPPINESS DEPENDS ON EMOTIONAL INTELLIGENCE

Of course, living in alignment is easier said than done. Behaving in ways that are consistent with values requires that we manage our thoughts, emotions, and outward actions in a positive way. Daily life offers many road mines that can cause irrational thinking and destructive emotions. Those in turn can lead to negative behavior or distract us from taking positive actions. If we want to be in charge of our behavior, we need emotional intelligence. Emotional intelligence is often defined as "the ability to monitor one's own and other people's emotions, to discriminate between different emotions and label them appropriately and to use emotional information to guide thinking and behavior."[10] Emotional competence is the application of emotional intelligence that allows us to live in alignment in the presence of competing and difficult to deal with emotions.

Key to emotional intelligence and emotional competence is the ability to recognize what we are experiencing at any given time and that begins with *self-awareness*.

FREEZE!

One of the simplest and most powerful ways to cultivate self-awareness is to practice the Freeze Game.[11] When you use the Freeze Game, you declare a short time out from whatever you happen to be doing at the moment. Imagine you've just hit the pause button on the streaming video of your life. Then ask yourself these three questions:

1. What am I thinking right now?
   For example, what am I saying to myself inside my head? Am I thinking about a problem at work? A relationship issue? The weather?
2. What am I feeling emotionally?
   Emotions are words, not sentences; for example, I feel sad, excited, angry, frustrated.

---

[10] Andrew Coleman. *A Dictionary of Psychology*, 3rd edition (Oxford, UK: Oxford University Press, 2008).
[11] The Freeze Game was introduced to co-author Doug Lennick by performance psychologist Rick Aberman, Ph.D., his colleague at think2perform.

3. What am I doing, and what is happening with me physically right now?

For example, am I sitting or standing? Am I smiling or frowning? What's the look on my face? Is my heart racing or calm? Is my breathing pattern normal or accelerated? Am I tense or relaxed?

The Freeze Game is intended to help you become aware of your "experiential triangle," the constellation of thoughts, feelings, and physiological state or actions that defines your moment-to-moment reality (see Figure 6.1).

These three categories of experience are shown in Figure 6.1 as points on a triangle—the *experiential triangle*. Thoughts, feelings, and actions are interconnected and usually influence one another. For example, if I *think* about someone who was critical of me yesterday, I am likely to *feel* angry; my heart rate will go up (*physiology*), and I may clench my fists (*action*) at the thought of what happened. My feelings and actions may even set off a new cycle of the experiential triangle, perhaps causing me to think about being critical in exchange, which in turn stimulates new feelings, and so on. Why not try playing the

FIGURE 6.1   THE EXPERIENTIAL TRIANGLE

Source: Joseph LeDoux, New York University.

Freeze Game right now? You can jot down your answers in the Freeze Game Exercise Worksheet in Appendix F. You can also download a copy of the exercise from the book Toolkit at www.leveragingfi.com.

EXERCISE: PLAY THE FREEZE GAME

What am I thinking right now?

_____

What am I feeling emotionally?

☐ Angry   ☐ Helpful   ☐ Frustrated   ☐ Playful   ☐ Tired
☐ Happy   ☐ Sad   ☐ Confident   ☐ Scared   ☐ Excited
☐ _____   ☐ _____   ☐ _____

What am I doing and what is happening with me physically right now?

☐ Breathing   ☐ Heart rate   ☐ Muscles
☐ Jaw   ☐ Movements   ☐ Appetite

_____

When you played the Freeze Game, what did you become aware of that you hadn't noticed before? Many people are surprised by how much is going on internally and externally, even when engaged in a supposedly simple activity such as reading this book. Your ability to maintain a state of well-being depends to a great extent on making self-awareness second nature. That takes practice. And that means playing the Freeze Game dozens of times a day for at least three weeks (research shows that's the minimum length of time needed to establish a consistent habit). The more you play the Freeze Game, the more natural it will become to check in with yourself to see what you're thinking and feeling and doing. As you regularly play the Freeze Game, you'll probably begin to notice many benefits in your life. You'll develop a deeper understanding of how you really think, feel, and act, and that may translate into more positive relationships with family and friends, reduced stress, more productive behavior at work, and greater overall happiness. Of course, simply recognizing your experiential triangle during many life moments won't in and of itself make you a different person. But "knowledge is power," and self-knowledge is even more powerful. As you begin to recognize how you show up on a moment-to-moment basis, you can decide whether you're happy with your experience, or you'd like to change it in a more positive direction.

In addition to understanding your emotional state in a given moment, you can use the Freeze Game to identify patterns in your cognitive, emotional, and physical state over time. For instance, make enough copies of the Freeze Game worksheet (download from the book Toolkit at www.leveragingfi.com) to record your responses several times a day over the course of two weeks. Schedule several regular times each day to practice the Freeze Game, such as after a morning workout, in the middle of the day, and before going to sleep. At the end of two weeks, review all your responses and make note of any consistent patterns in your experiential triangle. For instance, do you tend to feel relaxed after working out, physically tense by the middle of the workday, or thinking about problems right before bedtime?

CAPITALIZING ON SELF-AWARENESS

The Freeze Game keeps you in touch with who you are moment-to-moment. The point of such self-awareness is to use what you learn to take steps to maintain or improve your level of well-being and living in alignment. But before you can leverage self-awareness, it helps to recognize how much control you have over your thoughts and actions. You don't actually control your emotions. Emotions are stimulants to action. The word itself gives a hint about how emotions drive behavior: E-Motion. In other words, Feel It, Do It. In fact, you are responsible for your thoughts and actions. If you're angry, you still get to decide what to think and what to do. Your response to emotions can be mediated by your thoughts. Instead of E-Motion, you'll make better decisions if you change that phrase to E-Think-Motion. If at any time you are not behaving as you would ideally like, you can choose to change your behavior in the direction of your ideal self. Try the following experiment to discover how much power you have to change your experiential triangle:[12]

- First, close your eyes and concentrate for two minutes on a memory of something that happened that really made you angry.

[12] Doug Lennick was taught this exercise by Fred Luskin (author of *Forgive for Good* and director of the Forgiveness Projects at Stanford University) and performance psychologist Rick Aberman PhD, Doug's colleague at think2perform.

- Focus your attention on what happened and who was involved, and think about that situation for two minutes.
- After two minutes, open your eyes and recognize what you just experienced relative to your thoughts, your emotions, and your physical being.

What you will notice, if you are self-aware, is that you thought about what made you angry. It usually was a person, and within two minutes you might have thought about how that person angered you more than one time.

You may also have noticed that your emotional state changed. You might have become angry again; or you might have felt guilt or regret. Your focus on your initial response may change how you are feeling emotionally within the two minutes. You probably also noticed that you were beginning to feel physical tension in your shoulders, your heart rate picking up, and your breathing becoming shallower.

Everything that happened to you was a result of what you were thinking about. As neuroscientist Jeff Schwartz points out, "Focus is power. What you choose to focus your attention on has power over your emotional and physical state."[13]

Now, take the exercise to another level:

Take a few deep breaths, close your eyes, and for the next two minutes, imagine that your brain is a radio receiver and that you have three channels permanently programmed into your automatic selections. One channel is the gratitude channel. The second channel is the love channel. The third channel is the beauty channel. For the next two minutes, turn on one of those channels. Depending on the channel you choose, focus completely on what you are grateful for, or whom you love deeply, or what beautiful aspects of life and your environment you most appreciate, for instance, mountains, ocean, desert, and so on.

When you're ready, open your eyes and recognize what you have experienced. If you're like most people, you will notice that your emotional state became much more peaceful. You began to feel love, began to feel relaxed, and began to feel calm. You might have thought about all the things you are grateful for; or you may have discovered that you

[13]Jeffrey M. Schwartz, M.D. in discussion with co-author Doug Lennick, May 25, 2007.

have a deep appreciation for certain people or natural settings. What you will surely notice is that your physiological state has changed. Your heart rate and breathing are slower, and your face is relaxed. You might have even noticed a smile come across your face. Once again you have discovered the power of focus, and the surprising amount of control you have over what you think and how what you think influences how you feel emotionally and physically.

These exercises help us understand how each component of our experiential triangle affects the others. Most importantly, they demonstrate that you can manage your emotions by deciding what to think.

YOUR BRAIN ON HAPPINESS

When you decide what to think, as you did when you focused on the gratitude, love, or beauty channels in the earlier exercise, you were in fact practicing a form of meditation. Back in the 1960s, meditation was frequently considered in Western societies to be an offbeat unscientific ritual practiced by Buddhist monks, the Beatles, or hippies living in communes. Today, thanks to considerable neuroscience research, meditation has gained its rightful reputation as a powerful tool for improving health and happiness. That's because brain scientists have recently discovered that practices such as meditation literally change your brain structure in ways that reduce stress, promote mental clarity, and enhance feelings of relaxation and well-being. A 2011 Harvard study was the first to prove that meditation causes physical changes to the brain. Following eight weeks of listening each day to a recording of a guided meditation, research participants' brains showed changes on their brain MRIs from scans taken before the meditation program.

Those who listened to the meditation audios reported feeling significantly less stressed after the eight-week period. Their MRIs showed decreased grey matter in the amygdala (which helps the body deal with stress and anxiety) and increased grey matter in the hippocampus (which controls memory, learning, self-awareness, and compassion). Researchers concluded that meditation builds brain cells, decreases grey matter where less is needed because meditation lowers stress, and increases grey matter in areas of the brain that foster increased concentration, learning, and memory.[14] It's intriguing that the hippocampus, the area where neurons grew the most as a result of meditating by study participants, is the part of the brain associated with one of the principles—compassion, and with one of the emotional competencies—self-awareness. Both compassion and self-awareness are necessary for living in alignment and, ultimately, for our level of happiness. The overall conclusion we can draw from this study and quite a few others is that meditation is a powerful tool we can use to "teach" ourselves to be happy. As we've seen, meditation is not a complicated practice. It's a matter of deciding what to think—it's a matter of choosing the contents of our experiential triangle. When co-author Doug was 24, and a new district manager at IDS, he knew there was something he did that other people he worked with didn't do—Doug always decided what to think. He discovered that he was unusual in that respect by accident. As Doug recalls, "At one of my district meetings, I asked my team what they had thought about on their way to the meeting that morning. Only 1 out of 15 people in my district could recall what they had been thinking about." That was when Doug realized he had somewhat of an unfair advantage over people who don't decide what to think. That advantage has paid off throughout his career. The year he turned 25, his district was the top revenue generator in the country. He attributes that success to teaching his team to think, and to think about what they think about. For example, he would coach team members to decide to think about what to say to a prospective client, and to think in advance about how they could help a client understand what they were trying to explain.

ASSESSING YOUR LEVEL OF HAPPINESS

Exercises such as the Freeze Game are extremely useful tools for increasing self-awareness of your emotional state and setting the stage for positive changes. There are also a number of assessment inventories

---

[14]Sue McGreevey, "Eight Weeks to a Better Brain," *Harvard Gazette*, January 11, 2011, http://news.harvard.edu/gazette/story/2011/01/eight-weeks-to-a-better-brain/.

that can help you become more aware of your current level of emotional intelligence, which is a set of competencies that promote personal happiness by fostering self-awareness and positive relationships with others. The Emotional Quotient Inventory (EQ-i 2.0) was developed by psychologist Reuven Bar-On, one of the pioneers in the field of emotional intelligence. The ESCI (Emotional Social Competence Inventory) was authored by leading emotional intelligence researchers Daniel Goleman and Richard Boyatzis. Both inventories are well regarded, reliable measures of emotional intelligence. However, the EQ-i has the advantage of including a "Well-Being Indicator," which combines information from measures of four emotional intelligence abilities to provide a picture of your current level of happiness.[15] The EQ-i Well-Being Indicator includes the following subscales (among many), which research shows are highly correlated with personal happiness:

- Self-Regard. Happiness is a by-product of believing in oneself and living according to your own values and standards.
- Optimism. In the case of setback and disappointment, the ability to recover and claim a happy state is contingent on one's level of optimism.
- Interpersonal Relationships. Well-developed relationships help shield you from the negative effects of life's daily demands, thus enhancing and sustaining pervasive feelings of happiness.
- Self-Actualization. Happiness comes from a willingness to learn and grow on a journey aligned with your values. Your level of self-motivation and feelings of an enriched life ultimately drive your life achievements and overall happiness.[16]

Results of these subscales are combined to provide an overall assessment of one's happiness level, referred to as the Well-Being Indicator. As an example, co-author Doug's EQ-i Well-Being Indicator results appear in Figure 6.2.

[15] If interested in using the EQ-i to assess your overall level of emotional intelligence and current state of happiness, contact the authors at think2perform (www.think2perform.com).
[16] "The EQ-I Model and the Science Behind It," *MHS Assessments*, https://tap.mhs.com/EQi20TheScience.aspx.

FIGURE 6.2 THE EQ-I WELL-BEING INDICATOR

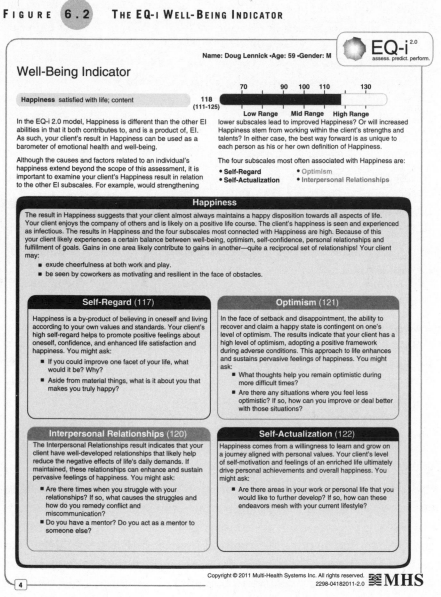

Source: MHS Assessments

CHARACTERISTICS OF HAPPY PEOPLE

Another way of helping determine your current level of happiness, and at the same time explore potential ways to increase your happiness, is to compare yourself to demonstrably happy people. Take a look at the following list of characteristics typical of the happiest people. These qualities are based on an enormous body of research.[17] How many of these characteristics are true of you?

- Routinely express gratitude for what they have
- Feel optimistic about the future
- Reach out to provide help to others, including co-workers and strangers
- Appreciate living in the moment
- Spend substantial time with family and friends, deepening and enjoying such relationships
- Engage in physical exercise on a regular basis
- Strongly commit to long-term goals
- Demonstrate composure and strength when facing difficult life circumstances[18]

It's useful to reflect on which of these characteristics are qualities that describe you, because those are strengths you'll want to protect to maintain a high level of well-being. It's also important to make note of any characteristics of the happiest people that you lack, because these characteristics represent attitudes and behaviors that you can actively develop to increase your level of happiness.

PLANNING TO BE HAPPY

It's not a coincidence that the happiest people tend to set goals for the long term. The happiest people don't necessarily just set goals to be happy. They often find much happiness in setting long-term financial goals, goals for future adventures, goals for a major career change, and goals for future physical accomplishments such as a triathlon. That said, one of the most satisfying life goals you can set for yourself is a goal to be happy. You deserve to be happy. Everything you do to live in alignment with principles and values will automatically help you be happy. Because of the intersection of money, health, and happiness, setting and achieving financial and health goals will also go a long way toward increasing your happiness. However, setting a specific goal to

---

[17] Lyubomirsky, *The How of Happiness*, p. 22.
[18] Adapted from Lyubomirsky, *The How of Happiness*, p. 26.

be happy will open you up to the possibility of even greater well-being. So, begin by thinking about the characteristics of the happiest people listed above as potential key activities for achieving your goal to be happy. Then review the key happiness-promoting activities and practices discussed next.

KEY ACTIVITIES AND PRACTICES FOR BEING HAPPY
Practicing Gratitude

Some people roll their eyes when they read an article or see a Facebook post that encourages them to "practice gratitude." Practicing gratitude may seem hokey. If you thought the earlier exercise which included tuning into the "gratitude channel" was a little silly, that's understandable. But, in the words of the nineteenth-century poet, Samuel Taylor Coleridge, try to "suspend disbelief," because there is a lot of research confirming the benefits of developing an "attitude of gratitude." For example, Dr. Robert Emmons, the world's leading authority on gratitude, has conducted numerous studies on the connection between gratitude and well-being. According to Dr. Emmons, "grateful people experience higher levels of positive emotions such as joy, enthusiasm, love, happiness, and optimism, and that the practice of gratitude as a discipline protects a person from the destructive impulses of envy, resentment, greed, and bitterness."[19] Other research shows that gratitude improves self-esteem and fosters resilience. Gratitude also benefits physical health, and even helps people sleep better.[20]

So how do you practice gratitude? Try one of the following activities:

* **Tune into the Gratitude Channel.** We suggested this practice previously as an experiment to demonstrate the power of the mind to change attitude, improve your physiological state, and manage difficult emotions. But "tuning into the gratitude channel" is

---

[19]Robert A. Emmons, *Thanks!: How the New Science of Gratitude Can Make You Happier* (Boston: Houghton Mifflin Harcourt, 2007).
[20]Amy Morin, "7 Scientifically Proven Benefits of Gratitude That Will Motivate You to Give Thanks Year Round," Forbes.com, November 23, 2014, https://www.forbes.com/sites/amymorin/2014/11/23/7-scientifically-proven-benefits-of-gratitude-that-will-motivate-you-to-give-thanks-year-round/#35b2ab56183c.

even more effective when used on a regular basis to promote a state of emotional well-being. Choose a specific time each day or several times a week to think about one or more people or life circumstances for which you are grateful and reflect on why you are grateful.

- **Keep a Gratitude Journal.** If you like to write, choose a time of day when you can take up to 15 minutes to write down three to five things for which you are grateful. Dr. Lyubomirsky's research indicates that it's often most effective to do this once a week rather than more frequently, so that the impact doesn't wear off.[21] But you may find it personally more beneficial to write in a gratitude journal every day. Other research suggests that spending up to 15 minutes writing in a gratitude journal right before going to bed each night improves the quality of sleep.

- **Express Gratitude to Others.** Martin Seligman studied the well-being benefits of writing and hand-delivering a letter of gratitude to someone who was especially appreciated. Research participants who completed this activity experienced large increases in their sense of well-being, an effect which lasted even a month after the gratitude visit.[22] This is an activity you can plan to do on a regular basis. Not only will you feel better; expressing gratitude directly to someone is bound to increase their happiness as well.

Building Optimism

Like practicing gratitude, deliberately cultivating optimism may seem a little clichéd. When things are tough, we may be annoyed to hear someone tell us to "Look on the bright side." But it's a fact that happy people focus on what's going well rather than on what's not going well in daily life. Cultivating optimism has an important benefit beyond feeling upbeat. To achieve happiness, you need to know what you want for yourself (WDYWFY), and you need faith that it's possible to get what you need and want. When you are optimistic about the future, you're much more likely to set goals for the future and more willing to

---

[21] Lyubomirsky, *The How of Happiness,* p. 96.
[22] Seligman, M.E., et al. "Empirical Validation of Interventions," *American Psychologist* (July–Aug. 2005): Vol. 60, No. 1, pp. 410–421.

make the effort needed to achieve such goals. That's why emphasizing the positive may turn out to be a key activity in your happiness plan. Try this practice to build optimism.

Visualize Your Best Future Self. Once a week or so, put yourself in a relaxed state, and spend 5 or 10 minutes imagining the best possible future for yourself. If you enjoy writing, you can write out your vision of your best future self, either after, or instead of, the visualization exercise. Doing this on a regular basis has been shown to produce increases in feelings of well-being up to several weeks after the exercise. Some research has also found that people who engage in this activity report feeling physically healthier months afterward.[23]

Practicing Acts of Kindness

One of the most consistent findings in happiness research is that the happiest people have the best relationships with others. Satisfying social connections are also strongly associated with longevity. To have good relationships, we need to be compassionate, which we demonstrate by showing kindness and caring to others. Compassion is one of the universal principles, and it's well recognized in the teachings of the world's major religions. The current Dalai Lama of Tibetan Buddhism is famous for this saying: "If you want others to be happy, practice compassion. If you want to be happy, practice compassion." In the Jewish faith, there is the concept of a "mitzvah," which means to do a good deed or perform an act of kindness. In the Kabbala tradition of Judaism, one of the main teachings is that "the world is built on kindness." In the Christian churches, kindness is considered an important virtue, closely linked to charity, which emphasizes the idea of showing love rather than just talking about it. In the Quran, the holy book of Islam, Muslims are taught to be kind to all of creation, including parents, children, neighbors, and animals.[24] In the last few years in the United States, the idea of "practicing random acts of

[23] King, Laura. "The Health Benefits of Writing about Life Goals," *Personality and Social Psychology Bulletin* (July 2001), Vol. 27, pp. 798–807.
[24] As explained in Homaira Shifa, "Kindness in Islamic Beliefs," *People of Our Everyday Life*, http://peopleof.oureverydaylife.com/kindness-islamic-beliefs-3704.html. Retrieved on May 31, 2017.

kindness" has become popular. These practices usually involve small acts of generosity, such as paying for the coffee order of the stranger behind you in the Starbuck's drive-through lane or putting money in a parking meter about to expire.

THANKSGIVING ACT OF KINDNESS

For a number of years Doug would take his son Al with him to a mid-scale restaurant on Thanksgiving Day. There would always be some people eating alone, often because they didn't have friends or family who invited them for dinner. Doug would go up to the cashier and tell him or her that he wanted to pay for dinner for everyone who was eating alone. Doug did this in the spirit of practicing acts of kindness, and in alignment with his value of serving others. He also wanted his son Al to recognize how lucky they were as a family, and how much they had to be thankful for. Doug also hoped this tradition would encourage Al to practice acts of kindness as he grew up.

There is considerable anecdotal evidence that such acts of kindness give pleasure to the person performing them. But there's a catch: According to research, such small acts of kindness may not increase your happiness level unless you perform a number of acts of kindness in the same day. If you spread out your acts of kindness, say one act every day or so, you're not likely to experience a happiness boost.[25]

That doesn't mean you should rule out performing occasional random acts of kindness, since they're likely to benefit or please the recipient. But if you want to experience a sustained level of greater happiness, it's best to find more substantial ways to demonstrate compassion.

Volunteer. One of the best ways to practice kindness is through regular involvement in volunteer activities. To reap all the rewards of volunteering, choose events or organizations related to a cause you really care about. Find opportunities that take advantage of your skills or will allow you to learn new skills that interest you. Find a setting

---

[25]Lyubomirsky, *The How of Happiness*, p. 127.

that is consistent with your personality or social needs. A few years ago, Linda, a lifelong New Yorker, retired to a small beach town in Florida. She started volunteering at the gift shop of a historical lighthouse as a way of trying to connect with her new Florida community. During her weekly shift, she was the only person staffing the dark and airless shop, and visitors were scarce. She quit after two weeks because she felt bored, claustrophobic, and lonely. A friend introduced Linda to a research project for which each week a group of volunteers spent a morning going up and down 10 miles of beach trying to spot an endangered species of whales and recording weather and ocean traffic conditions that could affect them. Linda became a conscientious member of the team. The project connected to her values, which included love of animals and appreciation of nature. As a bonus, Linda became friends with several other volunteers. By the end of the project, Linda was a lot happier. She felt better about herself because she had contributed to a meaningful cause. She enjoyed her hours on the beach in the company of friendly people who shared many of her values. Even though she was practicing kindness, Linda felt almost selfish because she was having such a good time. But as co-author Doug says, "Goal achievement, which includes being happy, is a rightfully selfish process, provided the goals are aligned with principles and values."

Practicing Forgiveness

One of the biggest barriers to happiness is holding on to anger about harm done to us by others. Another less well-understood obstacle to well-being is inability to forgive ourselves—when we hold onto disappointment about ways in which we have failed others or made mistakes that clash with our ideal self. The only cure for such unhappiness is forgiveness. We need to be able to forgive others for mistakes they've made, and perhaps more importantly, we need to forgive ourselves when we let ourselves down. In short, our well-being and happiness depends on putting the universal principle of forgiveness into practice.

When it comes to forgiveness, "Let it go" is a powerful mantra. Every day we suffer frustrations and slights that can irritate or upset us.

It's normal to have those feelings. But keep in mind from our earlier discussion of the body's stress response that every minute we spend feeling angry has negative physical consequences: When we're angry or upset, stress hormones elevate, our blood pressure rises (a risk factor for cardiovascular disease), and numerous other organ systems required for optimal health are negatively affected. That suggests that being able to forgive ourselves and others would improve not only our emotional well-being but our physical health as well. And in fact, many studies have found that the act of forgiveness can lower blood pressure, stabilize heart rate, as well as reduce depression and anxiety. When people do us harm or make mistakes, it's common for many of us to hang on to the negative feelings that their actions provoked in us. We remain angry or fearful, and the longer those feelings last, the longer we put our health and emotional well-being at risk.

As Doug often says, "Forgiveness is about giving up all hope for a better past." You really can't improve your past. But by forgiving yourself and others, you can go a long way to improving your future.

Pascale Kavanagh, a GenXer, shared her story of forgiveness with the magazine *Real Simple*. Pascale's mother viciously abused her physically and emotionally throughout childhood. Her mother continued to harass and berate her well into adulthood. Pascale's mother was a successful physician, a reminder that domestic abuse knows no racial, ethnic, or socioeconomic boundaries. After college, Pascale moved across the country to get as far away from her mother as possible, married, and in 2002 was fortunate to give birth to her own daughter. In 2010, Pascale's mother suffered a series of major strokes, which left her permanently and severely brain damaged. Since Pascale's father and brother had both died, she felt obliged to take care of her mother, a duty she didn't accept graciously. Initially Pascale felt rage, but after months of seeing her mother so incapacitated, her anger went away. Pascal just let it go. As Pascal says now, "I've become less interested in holding on to all forms of bitterness.... I see now that forgiveness is not so much about what you receive from people," she says, "but what you give them."[26]

[26]Pascal Kavanagh. "I Forgave My Mother for Abusing Me," *Real Simple*, https://www.realsimple.com/work-life/life-strategies/inspiration-motivation/stories-forgiveness#/abusive-mother. Retrieved June 20, 2017.

Practicing forgiveness of others does not mean that we should ignore our initial feelings of anger, frustration, or fear. In fact, in order to forgive, it's important to begin by acknowledging our emotions about any harm we have experienced. What forgiveness means is that we take time to process negative emotions caused by others' actions, and then move as quickly as possible to let go of the negative emotions stimulated by others' behavior. It's not necessary to forgive others because they deserve our forgiveness. It's important to forgive others so we can release the power others have to make us miserable, emotionally and physically.

9 Steps to Forgiveness

Fred Luskin, director of the Stanford University's Forgiveness Projects, suggests these steps for practicing forgiveness:[27]

1. *Know exactly how you feel about what happened and be able to articulate what about the situation is not OK. Then, tell a trusted couple of people about your experience.*
2. *Make a commitment to yourself to do what you have to do to feel better. Forgiveness is for you and not for anyone else.*
3. *Forgiveness does not necessarily mean reconciliation with the person that hurt you, or condoning of their action. What you are after is to find peace. Forgiveness can be defined as the "peace and understanding that come from blaming that which has hurt you less, taking the life experience less personally, and changing your grievance story."*
4. *Get the right perspective on what is happening. Recognize that your primary distress is coming from the hurt feelings, thoughts, and physical upset you are suffering now, not what offended you or hurt you two minutes—or ten years—ago. Forgiveness helps to heal those hurt feelings.*
5. *At the moment you feel upset, practice a simple stress management technique to soothe your body's flight or fight response.*
6. *Give up expecting things from other people, or your life, that they do not choose to give you. Recognize the "unenforceable rules" you have for your health or how you or other people must behave. Remind yourself that you can hope for health, love, peace, and prosperity and work hard to get them.*

[27] Fred Luskin, "9 Steps to Forgiveness," Forgive for Good, http://learningtoforgive.com/9-steps/, 2010. Retrieved June 21, 2016.

7. *Put your energy into looking for another way to get your positive goals met than through the experience that has hurt you. Instead of mentally replaying your hurt, seek out new ways to get what you want.*

8. *Remember that a life well lived is your best revenge. Instead of focusing on your wounded feelings, and thereby giving the person who caused you pain power over you, learn to look for the love, beauty, and kindness around you. Forgiveness is about personal power.*

9. *Amend your grievance story to remind you of the heroic choice to forgive.*

EXERCISE: FORGIVING YOURSELF AND OTHERS

Louise Hay, best-selling author and motivational teacher, recommends this exercise:

Sit quietly with your eyes closed and say, "The person I need to forgive is _____ and I forgive you for _____."

Do this over and over. You will have many things to forgive some for and only one or two to forgive others for. Then imagine the person you are forgiving saying, "Thank you." Do this for at least five or ten minutes. Bring your attention to all the resentments you still carry. Then let them go.

When you have cleared as much as you can for now, turn your attention to yourself. Say out loud to yourself, "I forgive myself for _____." Do this for another five minutes or so.

According to Louise Hay, "These are powerful exercises and good to do at least once a week to clear out any remaining rubbish. Some experiences are easy to let go and some we have to chip away at, until suddenly one day they let go and dissolve."[28]

---

* * * * * *

The practices described previously are just a few of the many ways you can increase your level of emotional well-being. Because money,

[28]Louise Hay, "Exercise Revenge and Forgiveness," LouseHay.com, http://www.louisehay.com/exercise-revenge-and-forgivness/.

health, and happiness are interconnected, everything we've recommended throughout the book leads to greater happiness. When we live in alignment and on purpose, we feel happier. When we work on key activities to achieve our goals, we feel happier. When we prepare financially for the certainty of uncertainty, we feel happier. When we exercise regularly and eat healthfully, we feel happier. Happiness takes work. As co-author Doug has said, happiness is an action sport. But if we take action, and do that work, we'll discover that the intersection of money, health, and happiness is a great place to be.

AFTERWORD

By Doug Lennick

Roy Geer would have been (and probably is) very proud of this book. Co-author Ryan Goulart and I and our collaborative writer Kathy Jordan are proud to have completed it for him and for us and for all of you.

You are responsible for your happiness, your physical health, and your financial health. The third has a lot to do with the first two. You can develop and leverage your financial intelligence, and we can predict that the results will be spectacular. You will be physically healthier, and you will be happier.

Kimberly King is an award-winning social entrepreneur whose many passions include promoting global health and well-being internationally and in the United States. King's experience working with projects such as the UN Sustainable Development Goals and Bhutan's Gross National Happiness initiative reinforces key messages of this book. In a recent conversation with Doug, she noted:

> *In nearly every culture, it's clear money does provide elements of comfort and security that generate well-being. Yet studies show that in countries where most can afford basic necessities, more wealth matters less than more joy.*
>
> *The same holds true for health. Once a fundamental baseline is achieved, the metrics of a good life are not measured in dollars or pounds, but in*

happiness and well-being. While money and health do matter, the path
to happiness is about having enough, not more.[1]

Michelle Young, who I introduced you to in the Preface, is a financial advisor who also sees the connection between money, health, and happiness. She states the following: "As a financial advisor I see that when people have a lot of financial debt and financial issues, it weighs heavily on them. When I help them get to the other side, I can see the relief emotionally and physically." Michelle's husband Tom, head of field distribution for Thrivent Financial, adds: "Happiness, health, and money are issues for everyone, and money is least talked about in a constructive way and has to fit into values like family and health and that leads to happiness. I really believe it's hard to progress if you don't have all three . . . money, health, and happiness."

Roy Geer grew wiser with age and could clearly see the connection between money, health, and happiness. In fact, as he aged into his eighties and neared 90, Roy concluded that a goal all of us share is to be happy. He also concluded that it was more likely that people would be happy if they financially could afford to meet their needs and if they were in good physical health. Roy himself was in good financial health and good physical health until a few days before his passing. Roy was happy and you can be, too.

We hope you've enjoyed the book and can put its contents to work. We also hope you pass the book on to friends and loved ones so that more people can develop and leverage their financial intelligence and find their own intersection of money, health, and happiness.

[1] Kimberly King in discussion with co-author Doug Lennick, May 15, 2017.

Exercise: What Are Your Top Values?

Review this checklist of values. Begin by checking off the 15 that are most important to you. Then reflect and narrow that list to 10, and after more reflection, select your top five values. If you have an important value not on the list, use the blank spaces below to record other values. Don't rush through this exercise. Take some time to reflect on what really matters most to you.

☐ Adventure	☐ Autonomy	☐ Challenges	☐ Change
☐ Community	☐ Competence	☐ Competition	☐ Cooperation
☐ Creativity	☐ Decisiveness	☐ Diversity	☐ Ecology/Environment
☐ Education	☐ Ethics	☐ Excellence	☐ Excitement
☐ Fairness	☐ Fame	☐ Family	☐ Flexibility
☐ Freedom	☐ Friendship	☐ Happiness	☐ Health
☐ Helping Others	☐ Honesty	☐ Independence	☐ Integrity
☐ Leadership	☐ Loyalty	☐ Meaningful Work	☐ Money
☐ Order	☐ Philanthropy	☐ Play	☐ Pleasure
☐ Power	☐ Privacy	☐ Recognition	☐ Relationships
☐ Religion	☐ Safety	☐ Security	☐ Service
☐ Spirituality	☐ Status	☐ Wealth	☐ Work
☐ _____	☐ _____	☐ _____	☐ _____

You can download a copy of this exercise from the Leveraging Your Financial Intelligence Toolkit at www.leveragingfi.com.

Exercise: Values and Behavior Alignment

Step 1: In Column A, rank order from 1 to 10 the values you most want your life to represent.

Step 2: In Column B, rank order these values from 1 to 10 based on time and energy invested in each over the last year or so.

Step 3: Determine the difference between priority score for each top value and priority score for values in action.

Step 4: Subtract number in Column B "Investment" from number in Column A "Importance" and place in Column C "Alignment Level."

Step 5: Reflect on alignment or gap between priority of values and time/energy based on each value. Is there alignment between what I believe is important in my life and my actual behavior?

Values	A: Importance	B: Investment	C: Alignment
	What I Want My Life to Reflect (Rate importance from 1–10)	Time and Energy I Spend (Rate from 1–10)	Alignment Level (Subtract Column B from Column A)
Wealth (how much money you have)			
Material Possessions (things you acquired)			
Family (as you understand your family, including non-traditional families)			
Social Status (degrees, job titles, awards, etc.)			
Health (physical and emotional)			
Power (feeling you control people and circumstances)			
Ethics (being honest, kind, generous, etc.)			
Fame (well-known by many people)			
Attractiveness (regarded as being beautiful or looking good)			
Work Performance (professional competence and mastery)			

How to Interpret the Values and Behavior Alignment Exercise:

- The larger the positive number in Column C (Alignment Level), the more you invest in this value relative to its importance.
- The larger the negative number in Column C (Alignment Level), the less you invest in that value relative to its importance. For instance, you may rank "Fame" as 10 in importance but 4 in your investment of time and energy. That leads to a gap of 6, which suggests that you may be spending too much time on a value that is not as important to you as others. As another example, you may rate "Family" as 1 in importance, but a 5 in your investment. The gap of −4 indicates that you may not be investing enough time and energy in your family relative to their importance.

- A score at or close to zero (−2 to +2) in Column C (Alignment Level) suggests close alignment between a value's importance to you and the time and energy you invest in that value.
- Such numbers are only rough estimates of alignment between values and behavior. However, it's a useful way to begin to think about how well you are using your time and energy.

You can download a copy of this exercise from the Leveraging Your Financial Intelligence Toolkit at www.leveragingfi.com.

Exercise: What Is Your Life's Purpose?[1]

Take some time to reflect on the questions below. Answering these questions can help you clarify the high-level meaning and direction that you would like your life to take. You may also find it useful to discuss your responses with a close family member or friend.

1. **What are my talents?**

2. **What am I passionate about?**

3. **What do I obsess about, daydream about?**

---

[1] Adapted from Richard Leider, *Repacking Your Bags: Lighten Your Load for the Rest of Your Life* (San Francisco: Berrett-Koehler Publishers, 1995).

4. What do I wish I had more time to put energy into?

5. What needs doing in the world that I'd like to put my talents to work on?

6. What are the main areas in which I'd like to invest my talents?

7. What environments or settings feel most natural to me?

8. In what work and life situations am I most comfortable expressing my talents?

You can download a copy of this exercise from the Leveraging Your Financial Intelligence Toolkit at www.leveragingfi.com.

Exercise: Visualize Yourself Living Your Purpose[2]

- Sit or lie down in a relaxing spot.
- Take some deep breaths, and focus in turn on each part of your body from head to toe, allowing your muscles to loosen and relax as you concentrate on each part of your body.
- While continuing to breathe naturally, imagine yourself near the end of your life.
- Reflect on your life to this point in time. Throughout the years, what has given your life the most meaning and purpose?
- Allow yourself to feel a sense of contentment as you realize that you are fulfilling your purpose.

[2]Based on an exercise discussed by Jim Loehr in his book, *The Only Way to Win: How Building Character Drives Higher Achievement and Greater Fulfillment in Business and Life* (New York: Hyperion, 2012).

- After spending a few minutes in reflection, open your eyes and return to the present while maintaining a sense of satisfaction about a life well-lived.

You can download a copy of this exercise from the Leveraging Your Financial Intelligence Toolkit at www.leveragingfi.com.

APPENDIX E

Goal Achievement Planning

PART I: TURNING WANTS INTO GOALS

There are many things we want in life, but to have them, we need to understand what we must do to achieve them. To turn *wants* into *goals*, *wants* must pass the "acid test." That means we need to decide if we can afford the time and resources required to achieve what we want, and are willing to spend the time, invest in the resources, and make the sacrifices required to get what we want. If we are, then we have a good chance of achieving our goal. If we aren't willing or able to do what's required to get what we want, then what we want should be considered a dream, not really a goal.

There can be many good reasons why you should defer a desired goal. Most importantly, you need to prioritize potential goals based on principles and your values. For example, if your top value is "Family Happiness," you may need to postpone training for your Adventure-fueled desire to climb Mt. Everest, which would take you away from your family for extended periods of time. You also need to

140

be realistic about your capacity to work on multiple goals at the same time. Everything you want may be meaningful and aligned with your values, but your available time and resources may limit how much you can accomplish in any given time frame. Use the worksheet "Turning Dreams into Goals" to reflect on potential goals (What I Want), determine what you would need to do to accomplish each goal (Key Activities), and decide whether you can and will do what it takes to make what you want a reality (The Acid Test.) If so, you've identified a real goal. If not, you can apply the acid test for a given want at a future time.

Part I: Turning Wants Into Goals

What I Want...	Key Activities *"Must Do" actions needed to accomplish this goal.*	Does What You Want Pass the Acid Test? *Can I and will I do all it takes to turn this want into a goal?*
Financially:	• • • •	
For My Health:	• • • •	
For My Overall Happiness:	• • • •	
Other Want:	• • • •	

Part II: Goal Achievement Plan

Use the Goal Achievement Plan worksheet to document your plans to accomplish goals that pass the acid test. This worksheet will help you develop, implement, and track progress toward achieving your goals. Once you've mapped out your goal achievement plan, put your next steps into your calendar and get started!

Part II: Goal Achievement Plan

My Goal:		
Key Activities "I Must Do":		
Resources I Need to Perform My Key Activities:		
People I Need to Support Me and How	Name	Support I'll Request
How I'll Track Progress		
How I'll Manage Emotions		

You can download a copy of the "Turning Wants Into Goals" and the "Goal Achievement Plan" worksheets from the Leveraging Your Financial Intelligence Toolkit at www.leveragingfi.com.

Exercise: Play the Freeze Game

What am I thinking right now? _____

_____

What am I feeling emotionally?

☐ Angry ☐ Helpful ☐ Frustrated ☐ Playful ☐ Tired
☐ Happy ☐ Sad   ☐ Confident   ☐ Scared   ☐ Excited
☐ _____ ☐ _____ ☐ _____

What am I doing and what is happening with me physically right now?

☐ Breathing ☐ Heart rate ☐ Muscles
☐ Jaw   ☐ Movements   ☐ Appetite

_____

You can download a copy of this exercise from the Leveraging Your Financial Intelligence Toolkit at www.leveragingfi.com.

Index